Everyday Human Values

WHAT'S YOUR SCORE

JAGADEESAN

A Sterling Paperback

STERLING PAPERBACKS
An imprint of
Sterling Publishers (P) Ltd.
L-10, Green Park Extension, New Delhi-110016
Ph.: 6191784, 6191785, 6191023 Fax: 91-11-6190028
E-mail: sterlin.gpvb@axcess.net.in

Everyday Human Values

ISBN 81 207 2136 5

Published by Sterling Publishers Pvt. Ltd., New Delhi -110 016.
Printed at Saurabh Print-O-Pack, A-16, Sec. IV, NOIDA

Foreword

The rise of civilisations and consequently nations, are due to the ascendancy of economic forces, and their decline, to the degradation of human values. This force of decline that today is taking on the power of a Natural Law is applicable not only at the macro-level in the life of nations but at the micro-level in the lives of families and individuals.

The inverse relationship between ascending economic power and declining human values has littered the pages of history with the ruins of wealthy individuals, families, societies and nations.

This book may cause hardly a ripple in the ebb and flow of tides of human consciousness. It is but a modest attempt to prod individuals who pick it up to laugh at themselves, their follies and foibles and to hopefully create a tiny ripple in the pool of individual consciousness. If nothing else, it could be used by teachers of human values in moral classes to initiate topics of discussion among students.

Most of the articles here are those that have appeared on a fortnightly basis in The New Sunday Times, one of Malaysia's leading English Sunday newspapers. I am grateful to the Editorial Board of The New Sunday Times for having seen the value of placing an occasional positive message within the overwhelming pages of reports and articles covering every possible aberration of human nobility bearing testimony to mankind that articles relating to goodness do not sell newspapers as aggressively as those relating to negativity.

My thanks also to my spiritual brothers, George Heng and Ricky Liew and Sister Sudha Kudva for having come forward so readily to help bring this book to its final conclusion.

I pray that this effort will be of some use for my fellow men.

If you do find it useful and feel that efforts such as these are worthy, please write to me and let me know your views, comments and criticisms.

Thank you.

J. JAGADEESAN @ J. JEGATHESAN
Sathya Sai Nilayam,
24, Jalan Abdullah,
Off Jalan Bangsar,
59000 Kuala Lumpur.
Malaysia.

Dedication

This book is dedicated to

BHAGAVAN SRI SATHYA SAI BABA whose inspiration, motivation and guidance launched me into this incredible adventure of life ... searching for values within myself, to try to raise myself a fraction above the pedantic and placid, to make Human Values not a slogan, but a living reality in my life.

Mrs SELLAMAH JEGASOTHY, my mother ... for planting the seeds of values in the early years of my life, tending the tender shoot with love and care to where it can offer today a few fruits of value to others.

SHANTI, my wife ... whose love has helped me search often my own conscience for a formula for a rich and understanding family life.

My children — **JEGATHEVA, ANASUYA, JEGATHEVI, SAI BHANU** and **JAGANATHA SAI** — who must share their father so much with others, and often have to bear the weight of the "litmus test" of the values talked about. The struggle I know is difficult but I assure them that the treasure will be great.

Finally, all the family members of the **SAI BABA CENTRES** in Kuala Lumpur, the rest of Malaysia and around the world whose love and care have made me to try to rise above myself, and to try to dream an "Impossible Dream!"

GIVE AND RECEIVE

1 Look around and see the world
Can you see what's going on
Can you see and can you hear
The voice of children crying out

2 So let your hearts my Friends
Expand and fill with Love
And reach your arms my Friends
For those who need

3 For every raindrop that hits the ground
A thousand teardrops falling down
For every smile you see around
A thousand voices crying out

REPEAT:
So let your hearts my Friends
Expand and fill with Love
And reach your arms my Friends
For those who need

Song composed and sung by J. Jagadeesan as theme song for Launch of **"Global Co-operation for a better world programme"** at Shangrila Hotel by YAB Datin Seri Dr Siti Hasmah. Song was offered as dedication to Dato' Seri Dr Mahathir Mohamad and Datin Seri, the Honourable Prime Minister of Malaysia and wife, for their contribution to Nation Building.

Human Values For Daily Living

(A proposal for a series of fortnightly articles in the media)

The erosion of the Human Values of Truth, Right Conduct, Peace, Love, Non-Violence, Respect for Parents, Elders and Authority, for Morality, etc, is leading to the decay of the moral and social fabric of societies at a speed never before witnessed in the history of civilisation. Malaysia, exposed to the negativity of external influences through the media of the newspaper, films, TV and video, is also a victim to this rising tide of erosion.

The "Future Shock" syndrome promulgated by Toffler is a reality as society is unable to withstand the speed of change being introduced by external forces and internal decay.

The newspaper, a media that often appears to appeal to the baser instincts of man by sensationalising sex, misconduct, violence and the moral decay of those "worshipped" by many because of their prominence in the world of films, songs or politics, can also appeal to the higher instincts of man and help in the reintroduction of forgotten values, of ideas that have been lost through non-use, of thoughts that have been distorted by misinformation and misinterpretation.

The proposal is that the media carry, on a fortnightly basis, cartoons and articles that will focus on the great human values of man that have been fostered by the teachings of the great leaders of the world and by the spiritual lights that have promoted the higher thoughts of man.

The articles will be totally non-sectarian, promoting no particular religion or religious belief. They will be designed to project the common values of mankind and to show the unity that can bind man together through the adherence to values and ideals such as Truth, Right Conduct, Peace, Love, Non-Violation, Respect for parents, elders, leaders, Dedication to work, etc.

Nothing in any of the articles will be designed to bring down or demean any school of thought. Everything only to elevate.

Note:

This was the introductory note that was sent to the New Straits Times that saw the beginning of a series of fortnightly articles that appeared for 1½ years.

The Problem

There is a "social" law, almost akin to a natural law that is now pervading humanity. The law of gravity is a natural law which posits the truth that if an object is dropped it must fall, unless a force is exerted to cancel or counter the force of gravity. This law is a natural law that operates in any country at any time regardless of race, religion or nationality

Today, a social law appears to be gathering to itself the awesome power of a natural law! It appears as though as economic development, as modernisation, increases in any country, human values must decline. This is a frightening phenomenon, i.e. that there appears to be an inverse relationship between modernisation and human values.

The critical questions that face modern man, that confront all Governments, political, religious and social leaders is this "as modernisation increases, must human values decline? Can human values be maintained? Can human values in fact be increased after the initial decline that has taken place?"

Since the practice of the highest human values is the core of all religions, one can perhaps use *belief in religion* or God as a criterion to measure the existence or degradation of human values .

Some time ago in October 1976, there was a massive worldwide survey undertaken by the Gallup International Research Institute. This was a public opinion survey of seventy nations in six continents representing two-thirds of the human race. The object of the survey was to assess the happiness, ambitions, worries and problems of Mankind.

The result showed that countries that had a high percentage of people unable to afford food, clothing and medical aid had also a high percentage of those who believed in God or practised religion. Countries where the majority of the population were easily able to afford food, clothing and medical aid had correspondingly a dramatic decrease in those who believed in God or practised religion. These included countries like the United Kingdom, West Germany, Scandinavia and Japan. Thus it appears that an increase in material prosperity has brought about a decrease in religious propensity.

Startling, as it may seem, all the material possessions do not appear to give happiness, satisfaction, inner contentment, peace, etc. Thus the countries which provide the greatest material satisfactions are those with the greatest number of suicides, broken homes, divorces, mental breakdowns, juvenile deliquency, promiscuity, etc. The values of man, the values that separate man from the animal, the values that keep harmony within individual families, between individuals, within societies, etc, appear to be declining, thus causing disharmony and lack of peace.

What is the solution? Must man, after struggling to improve his material existence through years and centuries of endeavour, now see all this effort drained into a cesspool of human values degradation?

How is it, that human values degradation is taking place at ever more rapid rates, is more pervasive today than at any other time in human history? Why are values such as respect

INVERSE RELATIONSHIP?
MODERNIZATION AND HUMAN VALUES

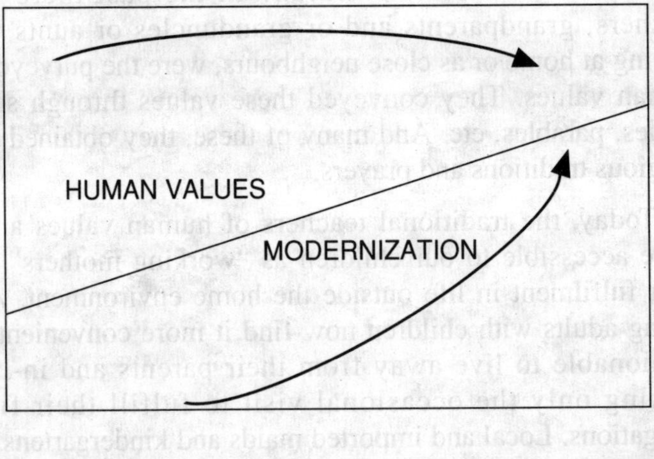

DEVALUATION OF MAN

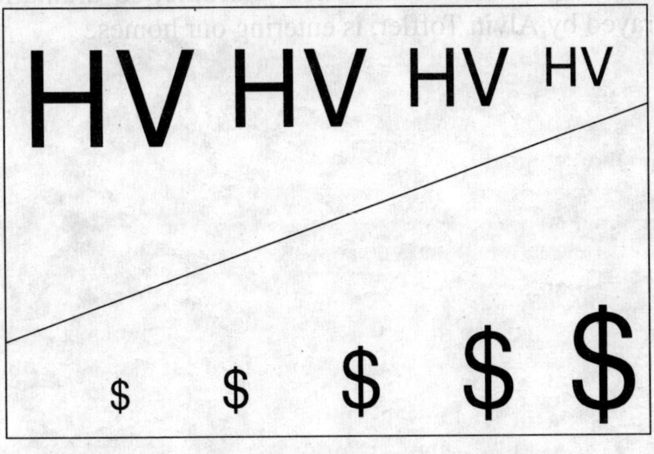

EVALUATION OF CURRENCY

for parents and elders, traditional practices, hard work, modesty, etc, being eroded so rapidly?

Let us look at modern homes. Who are the teachers of human values for the children? In the past there were mothers, grandparents and or granduncles or aunts who, staying at home or as close neighbours, were the purveyors of human values. They conveyed these values through songs, stories, parables, etc. And many of these, they obtained from religious traditions and prayers.

Today, the traditional teachers of human values are no more accessible to our children as "working mothers" seek their fulfilment in life outside the home environment. Also, young adults with children now find it more convenient and fashionable to live away from their parents and in-laws, making only the occasional visit to fulfill their fillial obligations. Local and imported maids and kindergartens thus become the substitute purveyours of family love and human values for a good part of the daily life of modern children.

Whilst the traditional bulwarks of human values education have been reduced or eliminated in the home enviroment, a "Future Shock" syndrome, so dramatically portrayed by Alvin Toffler, is entering our homes.

The Need

Whilst the adults of today, when they were children, had in their home environments, subconscious purveyors of everyday human values in the form of the mother, the doting grandparents, uncles and aunts who either lived under one roof or were neighbours, many of today's children, the adults of tomorrow, do not seem to have been given this advantage. Much of "family love" and human values are conveyed by imported or local maidservants and the Kindergartens.

However whilst Everyday Human Value inputs have decreased, the external influences on the minds of today's children have increased in geometric proportions. Let adults cast their minds back to the days of their childhood. To what extent and intensity were you exposed to values that were totally foreign to your own culture and upbringing?

The radio, the newspapers and the occasional cinema, possibly some friends ... they were the only ones who could have influenced our minds. Moreover, since the contact was not so pervasive, since the home environment had a stronger influence, we were in the main less likely to be attracted to things, ideas, habits and behaviour, foreign to our natural enviroment.

Today, the frightening phenomenon of *Future Shock* is becoming a reality in our homes. TV is bringing Terror and Violence into our homes. The VCR is bringing in Vice, Crime, Robbery and Rape. And it becomes a treat, an "all in the family" affair.

Would we allow a couple, our friends, to come into our home and make passionate love in our living room in front of our chidren? Our minds would shudder at the very thought. What a preposterous idea. Yet it is happening everyday ... in our living rooms through the medium of the TV and VCR. The adults watch with interest, the children with awe at these obviously modern and *avant-garde* behaviour patterns. Every possible deviation of human character is portrayed. Children rebelling against parents, husbands being unfaithful to wives and vice-versa, pre-teenage romances, cheating, lying, disrespect, etc. All these are enjoyed and video-recorded, in case we miss the programme.

In the eyes of the young child, whose mind absorbs everything like a sponge, the mode of behaviour being projected on the screen by the "much loved and admired" actors IS the modern way, and the parents and the child's behaviour are old fashioned.

Many of today's values, dances and songs are absorbed by the child through TV. Some parents bemoan the fact that their children do not know, love or appreciate their traditional cultures, songs, dances, ceremonies, etc. How can they? Have the children been given an alternative culture? Today we have a generation of children bound together by a "TV culture."

No effort is made to expose and teach the child cultural values, traditional songs and dances for their own sake as opposed to teaching these for some stage or tourist performances. Much of the culture and traditional songs and dances become thus reserved for the tourist and during occasional ceremonies, and not related to the natural environment of children and youngsters. Traditional culture and values thus have become dispensable appendages and not an essential ingredient to life.

Thus as TV and VCR bring Terror, Vice, Violence, Crime and Rape into the home, like the proverbial Camel they slowly push out Truth and Virtue (TV), Values, Character and Respect (VCR).

Does this mean that we have now to cast away all TVs and VCRs? Certainly not! Children's viewing of these must certainly be controlled and moderated **but more importantly** new bulwarks, new purveyours of Everyday Human Values must be consciously created, to act as an antidote to the negativity that enters the minds of the children.

Can such an antidote be found or must civilisation watch helplessly as modernisation creates a gradual erosion of Human Values?

How To Teach

The problem of teaching human values is as easy to understand, as it is difficult to teach. Just as one needs a compass or a knowledge of astronomy to navigate the oceans of the world and to avoid disaster, one also needs (and more importantly we need to give our children) a compass of Human Values to navigate the ocean of life. This compass is needed to help the child avoid the dangerous reefs of unrighteous conduct that can sink the ship of good living, or to be watchful for rough turbulences that can cause mental turmoil.

But how do you teach a child Everyday Human Values?

It is easy enough to teach a child history, geography or mathematics. One can teach the child that 2 + 2 = 4, or that a certain date is important in the life of one's nation and why. One can make a child understand where a particular country is located and its contribution to human welfare. But how do you teach a child the intangible aspects of Everyday Human Values?

What are these values we are talking about? Basically there are five fulcrum values which we might say form the fountainhead from which all other values can be drawn. These are TRUTH, RIGHT CONDUCT, PEACE, LOVE and NON-VIOLATION.

EDUCATION IN HUMAN VALUES...HOW?

For example, from TRUTH we have the sub-values of quest for knowledge, discrimination, self-analysis, curiosity, honesty, integrity, etc.

From RIGHT CONDUCT or RIGHTEOUSNESS we have dependability, courage, duty, ethics, cleanliness, gratitude, leadership, respect, etc.

From PEACE arises calmness, dignity, endurance, happiness, humanity, patience, reflection, self-satisfaction, etc.

From LOVE we have qualities of caring, sharing, compassion, dedication, devotion, generosity, forgiveness, etc.

From NON-VIOLATION we have the **psychological aspects** of Universal love, concern for all life, consideration for others etc. and the concomitant **social aspects** of appreciation of other cultures and religions, brotherhood, citizenship, national awareness, respect for property, social justice, etc.

It has been noted that the five basic Human Values arise from five domains of the human personality. From the PHYSICAL aspects of the human personality we have RIGHT CONDUCT; from the INTELLECT we have quest for TRUTH; the EMOTIONAL (mind) aspect relates to PEACE; the quality of LOVE arises from the "Divine Energy in man" and the quality of NON-VIOLATION from the SPIRITUAL or "Bliss/Joy" aspect of the human personality.

But how can these be taught to a child? Can these be taught and more importantly imbibed by a child in a classroom type enviroment? These are issues that have challenged the minds of the educationists, social scientists and religious leaders concerned with the serious question of degradation of human values.

Different countries in different parts of the world have struggled to find the ideal solution. Can human values be taught directly to children? Can it be integrated into the normal curriculum in schools and be taught through geograpy, history, mathematics, etc? Can it be integrated into cocurricular activities?

The other issue is, can it be taught within the formal school environment? And equally important, can it be taught outside the school environment by ordinary people, concerned citizens, mothers and fathers who want to make a positive contribution to nation building by helping to maintain and/or improve the bulwark of Everyday Human Values?

One particular Education in Human Values (EHV) teaching programme that I am personally aware of employs five powerful teaching techniques to convey Human Values to children. This programme — which involves dynamic thought activity or silent sitting, quotation and poetry, group singing, story telling and group activities — is being implemented by volunteers in numerous countries from South America to Japan, from Nigeria to Malaysia.

The children involved range from six to sixteen years — the most impressionable age in our lives. The programme is called the Sathya Sai Education in Human Values (EHV) programme, named after its originator Sri Sathya Sai Baba, the Chancellor of the Institute of Higher Learning (Deemed University) in India.

In 1994 the Government of Mauritius invited Human Value trainers from The World Sathya Sai organization to train teachers in Mauritius on the SSEHV programme. Similar training programmes have been conducted to teachers in schools in Phillipines, Hong Kong and Thailand. Human Values teaching programmes can be taught on a universal plane to all children, regardless of race or religion without violating sensitivities, but helping all.

Note:

Any reader who wishes to have details of this Sathya Sai Education in Human Values' (SSEHV) programme can write to the author for a complimentary booklet on this subject.

Truth

A parent asks a child to say that he or she is not in when answering a phone call — a seemingly innocent act. But that plants the seed of falsehood in the tender mind of the young.

If allowed to flourish and flower in an environment not concerned with promoting human values, the child may well in the future become a destructive element to the peace, happiness and well-being of family and society, and more importantly to him/herself.

Many parents, elder brothers and sisters, uncles and aunts are today responsible for planting these seeds of falsehood in a hundred everyday acts. They either encourage falsehood directly, or by themselves acting or speaking falsehood, they initiate and allow the growth of a vicious cycle of value degradation.

For the child in the drawing that you see, one lesson has been taught by the father ... "It is okay to tell a lie!" The next question is: "Where to draw the line? Who to lie to?" And like the man who got bitten by the snake he fed, the lie will one day rebound on the parent.

Why do we lie? There are numerous reasons:

(a) We lack courage to tell or face the truth of a particular situation.

Parents plant the seeds of falsehood in the minds of their children

What is truth? When?

(b) To save ourselves from embarassment.
(c) To protect someone.
(d) It is too inconvenient to tell the truth because it could lead to a lot of work or complications.

The reasons are innumerable! However, perhaps the lack of moral courage may be one of the predominant reasons.

When can we lie? Must we tell the truth under all circumstances? Let us examine one or two issues.

You are standing by the roadside. A girl comes running up to you and says that some hooligans are harassing her and she seeks your protection. So you hide her behind a bush. The hooligans arrive and ask you if you have seen the girl and know where she is.

What would you reply? To tell the truth and reveal her presence would be to precipitate violence. To say you have not seen her would be a lie! What would be the right action?

Readers are welcome to consider their perceptions on this issue.

Another incident. A family honour is at stake. A girl is to be married, but her brother is a current or ex-drug addict. It is likely that the knowledge of the brother's situation may endanger the marriage. You are a mutual friend. What would you do or say if the background of the family is being discussed with you?

Any views? To tell the truth ... or lie?

These are the Everyday Human Value situations we face. The fate of our children may well depend upon elders developing a right attitude to Truth and Truthful living?

Sometimes when the effect of you speaking the truth could bring sorrow or problems — would it not be more proper to remain silent?

It is said that if TRUTH has to be uttered — what, how and when it is said, could make the difference between TRUTH and compassionate TRUTH.

Perceptions Of Truth

We have seen how the seed of falsehood can be planted in the tender minds of children by a seemingly innocent lie. But the question now is, "Is Truth Absolute OR are there varying perceptions of truth?"

The classic story of perceptions of truth relates to the five blind men and the elephant. Each examined the elephant, or at least his portion of the elephant, and declared with great emphasis a statement that was absolutely true, as far as he was concerned ... the elephant is like a rope, a pillar, a huge fan, a huge pipe and a great wall. All were right or partially right from their perspective.

There is another interesting story of perceptions of Truth relating to a few people climbing up a mountain. At the bottom of the mountain the climbers could not see each other and thus as far as each could see nobody else was climbing this mountain. However, at the narrow peak at the top, they could see each other! They had all gone through the same experience, the same problems and hardships and were able to share experiences. Thus a sense of comradeship or friendship was created. There was respect for the other man who had or was making the journey.

SO! THERE ARE MANY ROUTES UP THIS MOUNTAIN!
I THOUGHT I WAS THE ONLY ONE... NOW I KNOW BETTER!
I WAS IGNORANT! NOW I CAN SEE THE TRUTH!
I AM THE KING OF THE MOUNTAIN! NO ONE ELSE IS HERE OR KNOWS ABOUT THIS MOUNTAIN!
I SHALL BE FIRST ON THE MOUNTAIN-ONLY I AM AWARE!
I HAVE THIS MOUNTAIN ALL TO MYSELF! ALL MINE!
PERCEPTIONS OF TRUTH

Life is often like that. The troubles and conflicts at homes, in offices, in society, in politics, in religion, in national and international life are because everyone clings to his perception of truth and does not take the trouble — like the blind men — to look any further. He rejects or refuses to look at the other man's perception.

Those at the bottom of the mountain are always in conflict and have little tolerance; those who have reached the top are more at peace with themselves and their fellowmen.

In the case of the blind men, if they had been "wise" blind men each would have been totally surprised at the claims of the others and they would have taken the trouble to investigate further. Then the real form of the elephant would have become apparent to them and each would have become the wiser for it.

Likewise in everyday life it is important that for every issue, every topic, every controversy, the mind should not be like a tunnel but like a radar. Those with tunnel mental vision (TMV) are always in conflict with others, not prepared to be sympathetic, or to listen to the views of others. Those with radar mental vision (RMV), have the ability to sweep the horizon of any topic, consider all options, listen to various views and come to a conclusion about what is truth, what is relatively true and what is false.

In our relationships at home, office or any other environment you will find that those with RMV are those who are relatively conflict-free and are at peace with themselves and their neighbours. Those with TMV can be easily identified by their intolerance and impatience with the views or ideas of others; they are not prepared to discuss or to attempt to see the other view point. Often the issue of right or wrong does not arise. One may disagree after seeing/listening to the perceptions of others, but at least you are now in a better position, if free from ingrained prejudice, to see the broader picture and decide on what is right action and what is true!

Are you a TMV or RMV? Do not point a finger at others. Look at yourself and to thyself be True!

Respect begets respect

The problems of the world today often stem from the fact that many demand to be respected without giving respect in return. This starts from the individual, family, office or society and every other environment where man meets man.

Let us take the individual. How does respect beget respect for an individual? You must first have respect for yourself, your appearance, your work, etc. before others can respect you.

If you go to a particular function which requires a particular dress code, and you dress in an inappropriate manner, it is a signal to others that you do not respect the occasion or those participating in the event. This may not have been your intention. You may feel that you have the right to dress as you like, but you have violated the rights of your host or other participants.

The fact that the host is civilized enough, has enough of his own self-respect not to throw you out may well be the reason for your continued acceptance in the function ... or perhaps you are rich and powerful, but nonetheless you have demeaned yourself.

Respect begets respect

From individual to family: If a husband is a wife-beater, does not respect his marriage vows as husband or father, does he have the right to expect respect from his wife or children? The problem of family breakups often stems from this lack of respect of husband for wife and vice-versa.

Likewise in an office environment. Here there is a formal structure. You are expected to respect your boss, the alternative being to lose your job, get transferred or be shelved. Respect in an office environment manifests itself in a number of ways.

On one extreme is the subordinate who fawns over his boss and becomes the perfect "yes" man. He may think he is winning the "respect" of the boss, but on the contrary he is not only losing his own self-respect but often becomes the object of contempt of even the boss and butt of jokes in his office.

The other extreme is the one who is so scared of the boss that he fears the boss, rather than respects him.

Every boss in his office should ask himself one question: "Am I feared or am I loved and respected?" Perhaps one good test would be to ask yourself. "How would your employee or subordinate treat you if you lost your position or if they or you moved and worked somewhere else? Would they give you the same respect they are showing now?"

Officers holding important and even not so important jobs in government should also ask this question.

Today many senior members of the private sector come and show respect to you and tolerate all kinds of nonsense from you. "If you lost your job or got transferred to a less important post would they give you the same respect?"

The irony is that the expression, "He commands the respect of others" has nothing to do with commanding respect or demanding respect. In fact the secret of winning respect is not to demand respect. "Give and you shall receive" is the old adage and it is true today. Only by giving respect can you get respect.

In today's world many groups, be they racial, religious, political, social, etc. embroil themselves in endless controversy on the presumption that others are not giving their group respect. They retaliate in kind and thus destroy peace and harmony.

Go out of your way if necessary to make the other feel that you respect his views, his feelings, his sentiments and automatically you will get his respect! This is Everyday Human Values in action!

Right Conduct

Freedom of expression

"Your freedom ends the moment your finger touches my nose" was the statement of a British politician in defining the limits of freedom within the system of parliamentary democracy. In mature democracies this seems to have worked relatively well and thus freedom of speech has reached its full flower in the Speakers Corner at Hyde Park in the United Kingdom, where statements from crackpots to intellectuals, amuse many, irritate some but amazingly seem to provoke none.

But perhaps all that may well be acceptable in an environment where respect for feeling of others, be it elders, parents, political and religious leaders, is no more the norm of daily life.

However what about in other environments, those we may call "the less mature democracies" (for want of a better term) or in traditional societies where tradition, courtesy, respect, softness of speech, etc., have become ingrained in the psyche and consciousness of the people.

In these societies, respect for elders for example and even the way one speaks to elders and others with respect, is a way of life. What if, in such an environment, full freedom is given to those bred in the western genre to speak what they wish,

Freedom of speech? How free?

without regard for the consequence of the words on the mind and feelings of others?

Can such freedom of expression, of the Hyde-Park variety, become an acceptable mode of practice in Eastern environments?

In the light of the circumstances of the Eastern and other "traditional environments" perhaps the limits of freedom expressed by the British politician regarding "finger and nose" should be transformed!

Perhaps a more relevant guide to freedom of expression in today's turbulent society should be: YOUR FREEDOM ENDS THE MOMENT YOUR WORDS PROVOKE MY HEART!

If the above is used as a guide for all — be it politicians, religious leaders, trade unionists or just the man in the street talking to his neighbour — then perhaps the democracy of nations can be preserved with love, harmony and respect.

"What is the harm if I speak what I think is right?" may be the question asked. "The other person also can speak his mind about me!" may be the generous offer. That may well be so, and it is likely that the person you are addressing your offending remarks to, may have a calm disposition and a higher boiling point.

However, this situation does not manifest in daily life, for normally there are others listening and often people only argue if they have an audience to play up to.

What if in the audience there is a listener who has a lower boiling point than the person you are talking to, and what if he is provoked to violence by your remarks!

It may be "poetic justice", in classic "democratic" tradition, if he vents his anger on the offending person.

However what is often likely to happen is that an innocent bystander, remotely associated by race, religion or ideology (or even none of these factors) becomes the target of unhappiness! After that it is too late to apologise or withdraw.

There is an ancient saying, that the wound of a knife can heal easily, but not so wounds caused by harsh words. That saying is still relevant today! Speak always softly and sweetly.

Thus an important Everyday Human Value to observe is "Do not do unto another what you do not want him to do to you." Somewhat a cliche but still very good advice.

Right Conduct/Love

Love for children and right conduct

No parent will say that they do not love their children however much they may neglect them or however harshly and cruelly they may treat them. Whatever the parents' true feelings for the children, there is one universal desire among all parents, which is that their children should be paragons of virtue, reflecting the best values of society, even though the parents may not be adhering to these values themselves.

The simple scene depicted in the following cartoon could happen in any home anywhere in the world. The mother (or father) indulges in slovenliness but expects the child to be clean and neat.

Any student of human behaviour patterns will tell you that this is an unreal expectation. Children learn by imitation, by copying the people they love and respect, be it a parent or any other.

Needless to say that to leave it to example alone would not be sufficient for most children and thus various degrees of firmness — discipline enforced with love and understanding — may be necessary. These may be necessary to overcome inertia in some children and over-activity in others. The river needs banks along which to flow and to benefit all. Without these banks flood and destruction would be the result.

However if authority and discipline are enforced without a concomitant attempt to set the example for such desirable behaviour patterns, then the result could well be smouldering resentment and the credibility gap between parents and children would be bound to grow.

A hundred everyday examples exists but these few may remind many parents of the need to set the example of role models for children.

If the mother keeps her bedroom in a mess and scolds her child to keep his/her room clean, this will develop anger and scorn within the child. "She does not do it. Why should I?"

The parents smoke and drink in front of children and yet advise them of the evils of smoking and alcoholism.

Parents talk ill and condemn their neighbours and friends, but chastise their children for being offensive to friends.

The list of examples could go on indefinitely.

Everyday Human Values, if we truly love our children, should spread from every individual. If that is done then at least the values have a chance to take root and have the opportunity to influence members of the family, neighbours, friends and society.

If your children do not respond positively to your example of love and Everyday Human Values, then discipline can and should be used.

And if even this fails and the child turns out to be the proverbial rotten apple, then at least the parents can have a clear conscience that they did their best.

That after all is what love and duty is all about — to do your best and to leave the rest to a higher force, destiny, fate — whatever.

Do not blow another's candle to make your own shine!

Right Conduct/Peace

Backbiting/Carrying tales

One of the most virulent diseases today, more prevalent and more deadly than cancer or AIDS, is the disease of backbiting and carrying tales. This is a disease that unlike the new AIDS has been around a long time — a disease as old as man himself.

This old AIDS, induced by "verbal indiscretion" (one might say), is "Assassination Induced by Defamation and Slander".

More people have suffered from this verbal AIDS than perhaps from any other disease — and sadly this is often infectious, transferred from mouth to ear, doing untold damage to individuals and families.

This type of AIDS is associated with, or more rightly, is caused by the absence of the EHV of Right Conduct and Peace.

When a person carries tales or backbites about another, condemning, criticising, and denigrating he does not realise that the hate and ill feeling he is generating damages him more physically, emotionally and psychologically than the person he is attempting to condemn.

There is a simple law of cause and effect — "as you sow so shall you reap". If you sow the seeds of peace and love — you will reap the fruits of peace and love. If you sow the seeds of jealously, hatred and ill will, you will also reap the same.

One cannot expect to plant bitter gourd seeds and expect to harvest a crop of juicy mangoes; to get sweet mangoes, you have to plant the seeds of that variety.

This cancer of dischord, hatred, jealousy, envy and ill will first implants itself in the mind of man like a demon seed. There it will fester and grow into a pus-filled wound, and will manifest itself in backbiting, condemnation, defamation, slander, etc. The person loses sleep, wastes time thinking and talking of the one he/she hates or dislikes and thus the cancer grows.

All must realise that by back-biting and condemning another, you only demean yourself — not the person you hope to demean.

All of us want happiness and peace in this life. The formula for finding that inner happiness and peace is not in trying to destroy the happiness and peace of others. **Only by giving happiness and peace to others can you expect happiness and peace for yourself** — there is no other formula, there is no other way; though you may search for these to the ends of the universe.

Normally this AIDS happens among relatives, friends, in an office environment, in political parties, or elsewhere where people ought to be united and mutually supportive — wherever there is a collection of people and where there is lack of love among its members. Do not become a carrier of AIDS, for who knows one day you could be its victim.

Peace

Peace is not a commodity to be bought and sold

"The absence of war is not peace"!

In today's society more and more people are finding the truth of this adage. The absence of physical conflict has not brought forth the inner peace that all men crave for.

What then is peace? For all mankind, for every individual, only the absence of mental turmoil can bring peace and with this peace will come an inner happiness and satisfaction in life.

If that is so, then we have to examine in what way we can overcome this mental turmoil and get peace. Inner peace, we all know, cannot be bought over the counter or traded. No external agent can give us this lasting inner peace, be it husband, wife, brother, sister, our position, wealth, name or fame. All these can give us some temporary happiness, possibly pride, but every person or object that can give us happiness has equally the potential to cause us grief and loss of peace!

Every person, is I am sure, very aware of this. Ask yourself, who or what was the cause of your most recent loss of peace of mind? Probably something or someone you cherished dearly.

"I want peace!" – The cry of every individual

If all those that are near and dear to us are unable to give us this peace, how then can inner peace be obtained? The answer lies hidden in the very cry of anguish ... "I WANT PEACE"! Very simple: remove the first two words "I" and "Want" and you are left with "PEACE". Let us examine this rather simplistic solution more closely.

The "I" refers to the human ego. How is the ego a robber of peace? Why do we get mental turmoil?

When someone says something about us that does not match with our own perception of ourselves then we get angry. However if the "I" in us is able to accept the adverse remark gracefully then we are not thrown off balance.

For example you think you are a great singer and someone says you croak. You get very upset! "How dare he insult my singing. When I can sing so well how dare he say that." The ego projects itself, anger results, possibly leading to hatred and loss of peace.

However, if that person is not a good singer and knows that or even if he is an excellent singer but has strong self-control and inner-confidence, and if a friend says "you croak when you sing", he will probably laugh and say "Don't I know that" and let the whole thing pass.

However in most cases the responses are "How dare he say that "I" am stupid, or "I" am incompetent or "I" am not pretty. It goes on. If the remark or abuse was **about another person**, you would join in and laugh for your ego is not affected.

Thus it is not the remark itself, but the fact that it was directed at you that is the cause of anger and loss of mental equanimity. However, if in all these instances, you do not project the "I" and just laugh and say, "Well, that is your opinion," then no one can disturb your peace. You have control.

Again, you have an expectation about someone or something. For example you may expect your wife, husband, children, or colleagues to behave in a particular way or produce a particular result. If that person fails to meet your expectation, you lose peace. The "I" has been let down ... and peace is lost. To recognise that this is the cause of your mental turmoil is the first step to reduce the hold of the monster "I".

What about removing "want"? Another great robber of peace is "Desire"!

Man today is caught in a frantic rat race of increasing "desires", increasing wants. Thus we work, we scramble, we cheat, to try to fulfill desire and if we do not get what we want (again the "I" ego factor) then we get upset or angry with the person or object that has prevented the fulfillment of that Desire.

How to overcome this is again to simply become conscious of this robber in your mind. Place a ceiling, a chain, on this robber called "desire" and slowly you will learn how to control him and not vice-versa. Please note that the secret is a "ceiling" on desires and not to be desireless or to have no desires.

It is thus said that the richest person in the world is the one with the least desires.

Thus we have the two robbers of peace — "I" ego and "Want" desire. Reduce the ego, the demands of the "I" factor and put a "Ceiling on Desires" and we will be on the right path to obtain inner peace and happiness.

Let's all give it a try anyhow. Good Luck!

Love And Peace

Do unto others as you would have them do unto you

"The smile you send out returns to you" ... this is a profound but simple truth, expressed I believe by the famous poet Omar Khayaam. And how dire is the need for all people to practise this in daily life.

Love is one of the greatest of Human Values, the one thing that is our birthright to have and share. Love grows and grows within you as you give and give!

Sadly, however, like the proverbial Shylock, many in the world today grasp this to themselves, distribute it in a miserly fashion as though giving this freely would reduce their wealth of love.

Many do not seem to realise that the more this love is hoarded the smaller it becomes and ultimately it will become mouldy in the darkness of one's heart, making the individual mean and bitter.

Unfortunately the word love has become a very misused word in the English language and often it is used to describe the more baser and carnal elements of human desire to the extent that many hesitate to use this word freely, for fear of it being misunderstood or made fun of.

The smile you send out returns to you

We have different ways to show love to different people. For our children and wife ... a hug and a kiss, loving words, and an occasional gift, may be necessary. But what about those whom we meet in our daily lives, especially in an office or social environment. Here we have daily contact with many people, some fleetingly, some for a while longer.

We often say "Yes, I like everybody". We avoid using the word "love", simply because we fear the word "love" or do not understand the manifestation of that emotion other than on a personal level between boy and girl, husband and wife, mother or child.

The question is how do we express that "love" or "like"?

There is a statement in the field of jurisprudence that goes as follows, "Justice must not only be done but must be seen to be done."

Likewise with Love. "Love must not only exist but must be seen to exist". A smile, a hello, an expression of concern of health and welfare, are but some of the numerous ways in which we can express our love for our colleagues, subordinates and friends.

If one has to manifest this great quality of love, the words of a great spiritual leader may well be a useful guide.

Love as Thought is TRUTH
Love as Action is RIGHT
CONDUCT
Love as Feeling is PEACE
Love as Understanding is
NON-VIOLATION
— Baba —

If our society is going to manifest any happiness and harmony, and if our material progress is to harmonise with our daily lives as individuals, families, societies and nations, then we should perhaps reflect on these words and see if we can make this love, this birthright of ours a living force in our lives.

It may be useful to examine each of the above values and see its relevance in daily life. This will be done in subsequent chapters.

not understand the manifestation of that emotion other than on a personal level between boy and girl, husband and wife, mother or child.

The question is how do we express that "love" or "like"?

There is a statement in the field of jurisprudence that goes as follows. "Justice must not only be done but must be seen to be done."

Likewise with Love. Love must not only exist but must be seen to exist. A smile, a hello, an expression of concern of health and welfare, are but some of the numerous ways in which we can express our love for our colleagues, subordinates and friends.

If one has to manifest this great quality of love, the words of a great spiritual leader may well be a useful guide:

Love as Thought is TRUTH
Love as Action is RIGHT
CONDUCT
Love as Feeling is PEACE
Love as Understanding is
NON VIOLATION
— Baba —

If our society is going to manifest any happiness and harmony, and if our material progress is to harmonise with our daily lives as individuals, families, societies and nations, then we should perhaps reflect on these words and see if we can make this love, this birthright of ours a living force in our lives.

It may be useful to examine each of the above values and see its relevance in daily life. This will be done in subsequent chapters.

Right Conduct

Elders set the examples: Children follow

A father (or brother, uncle or teacher) puffs nonchalantly at his cigarette and discourses with the child on the evils of addiction to tobacco. Families have cocktail bars in their homes well stocked with alcohol, all parties and functions are designed for "social" consumption of alcohol, (without which many consider a party not complete) and yet the children are warned not to drink. How many readers, your friends and relatives are guilty of this SIN — of insincererity to your children, of encouraging children to smoke and drink by setting the example, by being the figure the child wants to imitate.

A Child is no fool — he/she does not see the father drinking from the bottle marked "POISON" — but only from the bottle marked "BEER" or "VSOP". "Surely what is good for dad or for that matter mom is also good for me! Ah ha — they are trying to enjoy selfishly and want to deny me the pleasure ... so let me try it when they are not looking — after all there is so much around they will not miss anything". Thus opportunity makes the thief" and the child is introduced to possibly a life long addiction within the protective environment of the home.

Practice what you preach. Elders set the bad example and children follow.

Some parents have a remarkable way of justifying their action: "letting their children try it, so that they do not have to be introduced to this vice by their friends." Loving parents thus introduce their children to addiction and what is considered by many as a vice — "so as to deprive friends that opportunity."

It would of course be too naive to suggest that therefore all children of drinking and smoking parents are drinkers and smokers, and that all children of non-drinkers and non-smokers likewise follow their parents. In fact in real life we have sometimes found the reverse to be true.

Thus, obviously the secret formula is not in household addiction or otherwise. Naturally non-drinking and non-smoking by parents themselves are a strong moral and psychological force on the children, to likewise abstain. But in addition there is the need to build a strong bulwark of values that are inherent to the child and not merely influenced by parental presence. Religious teachings (as opposed to merely religious rituals) are strong re-inforcing factors that will develop love for God, and fear of SIN in the children.

It is often found that many children have dual value systems — one for home consumption and the other when they are by themselves with their friends. The critical test of a code of conduct, of a value system a child has imbibed is of course when children go abroad or into boarding schools to study, or live away from parents to go to work. Such situations will provide the real test of the moral fibre that parents have built in their children. Many parents readily claim that their 'good' children, have been spoilt by their friends and environment — forgetting that the parental environment is the one that children are exposed to the longest.

Communication with children is thus vital. They must understand the reason why something is wrong — not just told that it is wrong. They must be given sufficient education in Human Values at home or outside to develop their qualities of discrimination. They must be given trust and responsibility so they can develop early an attitude of living up to this trust and responsibility ... but most of all parents must live their lives as the role model they want their children to follow — if not they have only themselves to blame.

Love

"A friend in need is a friend indeed"

What a trite saying this — "a friend in need is a friend indeed." But how true ... and how sad if we have to find out who our friends are only in times of need.

What or who is a friend? There is a saying that "when the lake is full the frogs gather and croak, but when the lake is dry the frogs disappear." It would be very useful for all, especially the rich and those in positions of power, to look around them to see who their real friends are, who will still be around when the well runs dry.

How then does one detect a true friend from a "passer-by", the sycophants and opportunists. A true friend can be detected by his attitude towards you, totally unaffected by your wealth or status. He will not hesitate to tell you when he thinks you are wrong, his criticism will always be constructive; and though what he says may prick your conscience, and may even hurt your feelings, you will on reflection realise that he is doing this or saying this for your own good.

The friend will also praise you when you do right and also try to dissuade you from doing what is wrong for your position, family, health, welfare, whatever.

When the well or lake is full the frogs will gather around

Many people of wealth and position are unable to distinguish from the true friend and the "yes man" friend. In fact some, to their own future detriment tend to cultivate and encourage such "yes man" friends and keep away from friends who appear to contradict their views and criticise them for their own good.

The other type of deadly friend is the one who is determined to undermine the willpower and right-conduct of their friends. I have often seen so called friends, urging a friend who is trying to give up smoking, drinking, gambling or womanising, to join them saying "come-and-have a drink (or any other) just for my sake. Keep me company. What type of friend are you?"

Have you such friends? If you have, then think of the words of the famous or infamous Latin American guerrilla fighter Che Guevara, who called out to the almighty saying: "God, protect me from my friends, I can look after my enemies." How true this statement is for those fighting the battles of life against myriad temptations and vices. Indeed we need to be protected from misguided friends, for our enemies do not have the capacity to mislead us.

It is an excellent exercise in Everyday Human Values for each one of us to not only look around at who our true friends may be, but to also ask ourselves, "What type of a friend am I?" Are you one who thinks of the best interests of your friend?

Are you one who would, like the proverbial fox that lost its tail, encourage your friends to lose their tails i.e. whatever ideals and values they are trying to uphold? Are you the one who only befriends those who can do something for you in return and thus your friendship is no more than an exercise in barter?

Are you one who has the courage to try to dissuade your friends from negativity and if necessary dissociate yourself from those who would deliberately try to demean and degrade your values?

The world needs love in the form of friendship that cares and shares, that seeks no favour and harbours no fear — a friend who tries to elevate one to higher values of life and living. If you have such a friend you have a precious diamond.

or woman using, to join them saying "come-and-have a drink (or any other) just for my sake. Keep me company. What type of friend are you?"

Have you such friends? If you have, then think of the words of the famous or infamous Latin American guerrilla fighter Che Guevara, who called out to the almighty saying: "God, protect me from my friends; I can look after my enemies." How true this statement is for those fighting the battles of life against myriad temptations and vices. Indeed we need to be protected from misguided friends; for our enemies do not have the capacity to mislead us.

It is an excellent exercise in Everyday Human Value for each one of us to not only look around at who our true friends may be, but to also ask ourselves: "What type of a friend am I?" Are you one who thinks of the best interests of your friend?

Are you one who would, like the proverbial fox that lost its tail, encourage your friends to lose their tails i.e. whatever ideals and values they are trying to uphold? Are you the one who only befriends those who can do something for you in return and thus your friendship is no more than an exercise in barter?

Are you one who has the courage to try to dissuade your friends from negativity and if necessary dissociate yourself from those who would deliberately try to deprave and degrade your values?

The world needs love in the form of friendship that cares and shares, that seeks no favour and harbours no fear — a friend who tries to elevate one to higher values of life and living. If you have such a friend you have a precious diamond.

Truth

Practise what you preach

What is truth in the level of day to day experience? Philosophers may say that Truth is that which is never changing, unalterable by the ravages of time!

However, such thoughts of the sublime may not concern many at the everyday level of existence. Let us look at this Truth as an expression of Everyday Human Values.

One good definition of Truth is "that which exists when there is uniformity of thought, word and deed."

When a person, with a clarified consciousness and unconfused mind and intellect "thinks" thoughts based on Love and Righteousness, when he speaks as he thinks and when he acts as he speaks, one may say that truth is being manifested.

Unfortunately in today's society we find that many people manifest confused or negative thinking. Their speech does not reflect good thoughts and their actions do not reflect what they speak. Due to this society is filled with deception and falsehood causing misery to many.

When a teacher tells her or his children not to argue or fight with other students and is witnessed arguing and fighting with fellow teachers or worse, at night outside some

Practice what you preach. Parents lay the seeds of evil behavior in the tender minds of children

pub; when directors of companies pledge certain benefits to their shareholders or clients and then go out of their way to deliberately misuse funds and positions; when religious leaders preach of love and understanding needed for all humanity and yet at the same time condemn others; when politicians do not adhere to their pledges to their constituents, all these are manifestations of the degradation of the values of truth in society.

Why then does an individual deviate from truth? It is either because of greed, some self gain or because one lacks moral courage.

When a person wants something or desires to win some favour he does not genuinely deserve, then he may manifest untruth. .Likewise a lack of courage and fear of the consequences of truth makes many a liar in this world.

How often do we individuals who witness make fun of their superiors' actions or words behind their back, and yet praise those very actions or words in front of them?

The fact that they could choose to be silent does not seem to strike them as an honest option open to them.

Thus, it goes on in homes, in offices, in governments, in religious institutions, in political parties, man not manifesting consciousness of high thoughts, words and deeds. The result is that this mode of behaviour is adopted by youngsters and the vicious cycle of degradation of values continues.

However, all adherents of truth must also remember that the value of truth should not be used to undermine other great values like right conduct, peace and love. Truth should not be harsh, truth should not be used to demean and undermine others. Truth should be spoken sweetly and with love. If a truth will do more damage than good, it is better to be silent.

"To thyself be true" has been a statement that is time-tested and indeed we should be. But it should be remembered that the truth here is expected to be a value associated with higher thoughts. The statement does not say "to thyself be true and all else be damned." We should practise what we preach, but only preach goodness, love and harmony, for that is ultimately the highest manifestation of truth, for it is Love as thought that is truth.

Why then does an individual deviate from truth? It is either because of greed, one's self gain or because one lacks moral courage.

When a person wants something or desires to win some favour he does not genuinely deserve, then he may manifest untruth. Likewise a lack of courage and fear of the consequences of truth makes many a liar in this world.

How often do we find individuals who witness make fun of their superiors' actions or words behind their back, and yet praise those very actions or words in front of them?

The fact that they could choose to be silent does not seem to strike them as an honest option open to them.

Thus it goes on in homes, in offices, in governments, in religious institutions, in political parties, man not manifesting consciousness of high thoughts, words and deeds. The result is that this mode of behaviour is adopted by youngsters and the vicious cycle of degradation of values continues.

However, all adherents of truth must also remember that the value of truth should not be used to undermine other great values like right conduct, peace and love. Truth should not be harsh, truth should not be used to demean and undermine others. Truth should be spoken sweetly and with love. If a truth will do more damage than good, it is better to be silent.

"To thyself be true" has been a statement that is time-tested and indeed we should be. But it should be remembered that the truth here is expected to be a value associated with higher thoughts. The statement does not say "to thyself be true and all else be damned." We should practise what we preach, but only preach goodness, love and harmony, for that is ultimately the highest manifestation of truth, for it is Love as thought that is truth.

Peace

See, hear and speak no evil

There were once three wise monkeys – see no evil, hear no evil and speak no evil. As ancestors of man they tried to show the way for man to live a life of peace and happiness. However, man made one mistake – he assumed that the message was only for the monkeys and true enough monkeys today do not see, hear or speak evil ... that, they have left to man.

It is said that there are 4 types of people in this world:

(1) Those who try to discover their own faults, however small they may be, try to correct them, and only look at the good in others.
(2) Those who look at only the good in themselves and also the good in others.
(3) Those who look at only the good in themselves and only at the faults in others.
(4) Those who think that all their bad qualities are good points and try to find faults in the good others do.

Look at the accompanying picture and see if you can identify in which category the various characters belong to. More importantly, look at yourself and see in which category you belong.

Speak no evil, hear no evil, see no evil. The 3 wise monkeys can do it

Do not attempt to fit your friends into any category for that may make you slide down to the fourth category. Just look within yourself and try to elevate yourself to the first category and automatically you will be at peace with yourself and all your neighbours.

Many of the problems and discordant voices in the world arise because the world is full of fault finders — those who rarely look at the good but only at the negative and are quick to "pass the buck" of wrong action to others.

This starts at home for example, with the mother who is walking in her hall. Her daughter is lying on the floor reading a book with a cup of coffee beside her. The mother accidentally knocks the cup and scolds the daughter "Stupid child! Is that the place to place the cup?"

The next day the mother is lying on the floor, reading on the mat with her cup of coffee beside her. Her daughter walks by and knocks the cup and the mother jumps up "Stupid child, can't you see where you are going?" And thus the drama of the fault-finders continues, extending to offices, societies, religious and social institutions, etc.

A person in the fourth category — seeing, speaking, hearing, thinking and doing negative actions — can never be at peace with himself, for he cannot stomach the success, fame, wealth, position, etc. of others and will always be trying to think of ways and means to degrade the others — not realising that he degrades only himself with such thoughts, words or deeds.

The time perhaps, has come to replace the three wise monkeys with the five Children of Immortality — "SEE NO EVIL, HEAR NO EVIL, SPEAK NO EVIL, THINK NO EVIL AND DO NO EVIL."

There is a saying that demonstrates how we elevate or degrade ourselves with our own thoughts: "God if you think of, God you are, dust if you think of, dust you are, thoughts are things, as you think so you become!!" Let all of us try — we may not become Gods — but most certainly we can absorb and display God-like qualities in our lives.

Right Conduct

Children learn from parents/adults

There is a saying, "the people deserve the Government they get." Could it also be true that "parents deserve the children they get?" If the plant that emerges from the ground is weak and unhealthy and its fruits are riddled with insects, the fault is not the plant's but that of the farmer.

Likewise, if the teenagers and youth of today have deviated from cherished values of religion and spirituality, we must seek the fault not in the generation of youth but in the generation of adults that have fostered the youth.

Today, youth are being blamed for all kinds of negative behaviour and are considered by many as trouble makers and a problem to the nation. However, this is a wrong perception. The youth have great energy, talent, skills, aspirations and love, but very few adults are prepared to spend their time with the youth to help them foster this great reservoir of talents.

Tragically, on the other hand, this great store of energy and dynamism is constantly barraged with criticism and ridicule. And most damaging of all — negative role models. In simple words: Bad Examples.

Parents:– The greatest teachers

Parents who constantly show disrespect for each other; parents who only communicate with each other through snarls and howls, are only planting the seeds of disrespect towards themselves in the tender minds of youth. As you sow, so you reap.

Let us look at the picture — indeed a caricature of real life. But let us look at ourselves. Are we caricatures of the very negativity that we abhor? Some might say that the picture is an exaggeration. No child would ever speak to the parent like that! That may well be true but if you are the parent portrayed, can you imagine what is in the mind of the child. The son or daughter may fear to speak but they most certainly would not fear to think ... and herein lies the great tragedy.

A real life incident may be worth quoting and readers may wish to see "if the cap fits." A five year old child blurts out to her elder brother "shut-up ... bloody fool" or words to that effect. The mother promptly slaps the child and says "never use such foul language." But where does a five year old pick up words like that? The TV is one source, but her parents can point out that decent people never use such language. But what if the parent or parents are the source of such language!

The child's mind, like an innocent sponge that it is, absorbs the vibrations of its environment and then when the sponge is squeezed ... only the water that is taken in emerges. The fault here was clearly the parent's not the child's. Anyone of you readers find this a familiar situation?

Remember: "God if you think of, God you are. Dust if you think of, dust you are. As you think so you become." The ugly thought-seeds implanted in the tender minds of children will bear the same bitter fruits.

There are very few rare gems who are self-motivators. Only great "Lights of the world" live like lotuses, surrounded by mud and slime but never ever being affected by either. The majority of human kind are like creepers, clinging onto and growing round the first support they come into contact with.

There are different schools of thoughts as to what is the determining factor of the human personality. However, whether it is past karma (or re-birth), inherited genes, or environment, none of these schools of thought will deny the importance of parents as role models.

If you care enough to wonder what type of character your child will develop into, examine first your own lifestyle. Are you living up to the cherised values of your culture and religion? Or, are you a better example of "Do as I tell you but don't do as I do!".

It would be an absurdity for a farmer who has planted a lemon seed to expect the tree to bear mango fruits. The tree will only bear bitter lemons. Similarly, the child — the most tender seed and the crown of all creation — needs the most righteous and loving environment in order to be nurtured into a useful and self-respecting individual, a tribute to his upbringing and his nation.

Let all adults, before we try to correct the child, first try to correct ourselves ... the child will follow!

Right Conduct

Words and sentiments such as "Dignity of Labour", "To thyself be True", "Work is Worship, Duty is God" appear to be under seige by the corrosive forces of Human Values degradation.

"Minimum work for maximum pay", "Why work so hard?", "Don't show off by working hard" are the new slogans that appear to be creeping into the offices and workplaces of society. Sadly these sentiments are not just restricted to one level of the workforce. It is a malaise that seems to pervade at all levels where one does not hold direct responsibility or where one's work output cannot be directly measured.

Needless to say there may be numerous exceptions to the rule, but nonetheless the negative forces are creeping in.

Sometimes people feel justified not to give their best or to go that extra mile because they feels that they are not being paid well or not being treated well or given the recognition they think deserve. Thus he or she begins the great "goof off", tyring to get away by giving the least.

Every worker, be he wearing a white collar and tie in an air-conditioned environment or a blue collar on the factory

Work so that you can be proud of your moral integrity and dignity.
Work is worship. Duty is god.

floor, must search within his conscience. *If one does not do things in the world for one's own personal satisfaction; if one does not strive for excellence within oneself in the performance of one's task; if one is satisfied to wallow in the morass of mediocrity,* then one is merely eroding one's own self-esteem. You are the biggest loser, no one else.

If you feel the salary is inadequate; if you feel your promotion has been overlooked; if you are not being treated fairly, then leave the job and look for another that will give you back your self-esteem. However if you decide to stay in that job, then do your best for your own self-satisfaction, your own pride, your own measure of your worth ... then even if you feel unhappy about the salary or the work environment, you will at least be happy with yourself. This is the most important formula for one's own happiness ... self-confidence and self-satisfaction.

All workers, white or blue collared should ask themselves: "Have I inadvertently placed a cancer of discontent within myself that is now eating up my inner happiness and peace? Am I a living, walking cancer in my work environment, causing discontent among others, transferring my disease to others?" If your answer is "Yes!", then you must be a very unhappy individual.

Look at yourself in the mirror — fight the cancer of discontent with self-confidence and self-pride. Decide that you will do your best and leave the rest. Work as though it is worship with full devotion to your task at hand and you will find that you will become a happier person.

You will be happy, your workplace will suddenly appear more cheerful, your productivity will increase, others will begin to respect you, and you, multiplied by a few thousand, will benefit not only yourself, but society and the nation!

Harmony of thought, word and deed!

Truth

Speak as you think, act as you speak. This is the sign of humanity.

Harmony of thought, word and deed. This is the sign of the humanity in man, i.e. humanity at its highest level. However, harmony of thought, word and deed by itself is not enough. There is one step prior that manifests the greatness of a true man and differentiates him from the rest of humanity, i.e. the thoughts themselves should be noble, pure and righteous.

This of course is man's greatest problem. How to harness the wayward mind and make it go along noble lines? This is a separate subject altogether that we will tackle later.

For the time being, let us look at the picture. How many readers have found themselves in this situation? Where your thoughts were definitely in one direction and your actions in another, and most interestingly the mind is aware that the actions are against one's basic instincts, one's finer sentiments.

Sometimes of course, you cannot avoid this situation because of circumstances. A friend or colleague is going to go abroad, or is leaving the office. Someone decides to give him a dinner ... a dinner that the person going away reluctantly accepts because he already has too many dinners to attend. He needs the free time to do his own thing but social etiquette makes him accept. The hat is passed around, you know that the money you are donating for the dinner could have been better spent on some charitable project, yet you "cough up" ... the pressure of social etiquette.

Here is a situation where both the receiver and the giver accept a situation purely out of social etiquette and not for a social need. How wonderful if the person going away had called for a party to be thrown for the handicapped or disabled or children in the squatter areas. The monetary cost would have been much lower than in a hotel, and much happiness would have been created. An event of social etiquette would have also fulfilled a social need. Though this may sound highly idealistic, I hope those reading this will give this some serious thought and thus help to spread happiness a bit further. After all should we not live for ideals?

The event in the picture, however, does not even fulfill a need of social etiquette. It only satisfies a baser instinct of man — to "curry favour", to look good in the eyes of a superior and no "need" is being fulfilled.

Oddly enough when the boss invited the subordinate for the birthday he probably did it merely to be generous to his staff, not for presents. However, people often read other reasons for actions of their peers and take action that they think will please them.

Often man is caught in the form not the content of actions and deeds. Take the situation of political leaders visiting their constituencies or commemorating a particular event. The followers spend unneccessary funds on decorations, huge garlands, gifts, and the like all of which would have strained the budget of the organisers.

In fact most leaders attending such functions do not look forward to gifts and ceremonies, they accept it because it is given. **But no leader worth his salt should be offended if such ostentation is not provided.**

Leaders are given all types of souvenirs and gifts for launching or attending various functions, and their homes are often cluttered with such "junk". After some time such gifts become a burden not a joy. What is most interesting is that often the givers of these gifts go through lots of arguments on the need for a gift, the type of gift and whether they can afford it.

Perhaps, leaders and in the case of the picture, the boss, can help a lot by announcing in advance that there should be no ostentation, no expensive gifts. By this means they help the "would be givers" by removing the pressure of social etiquette.

Man is always caught in conflict because he is unable to harmonise his actions with his thoughts. Once man lives with high thoughts, speaks as he thinks and acts as he speaks he will achieve a considerable amount of harmony in his life.

Do unto others what you want others to do unto you

Right Conduct

Do unto others what you want others to do unto you!

Cynicism, back-biting, demeaning others ... this is a cancer, a disease more serious than AIDS that is destroying the moral fibre of man. Add to this jealousy, selfishness, and envy, and you have a virtual epidemic of diseases that are raging within the minds of individuals, of small minds who by their own words and actions demean themselves rather than the person they want to demean.

Look at the picture. Have you ever been in this situation? Many, I am sure, have been. Even if you have not voiced the words, have the thoughts invaded your mind? And worse, have you allowed your actions to be influenced by negative thoughts and words? If you have, reflect on your actions. What have you achieved?

Did you feel proud of your thoughts, words or deeds? Did you sleep easy? Even if you bragged about it among your peers, did you mention it to anyone you respected or anyone from whom you wished to win respect?

Consider carefully this quite typical office situation. You have been by-passed for promotion. Your colleague, your junior or someone from outside has been promoted or placed in a position above you. This position may be one which you feel you were entitled to. Alternatively, though you know you are not entitled to the position, you personally dislike the person who has been placed above you. What should you do?

As in the picture, if you begin to ferment discontent, discord and non-cooperation, this could easily "backlash" on you if your seniors know that you have taken this negative attitude. However, this is a negative reason for not perpetrating a negative act!

If you are entitled to the position then ask yourself why have you been by-passed? Perhaps, by some self-examination or honest (non-hostile) discussion with your seniors you could ascertain as to what was the reason you were by-passed. Perhaps top management does not appreciate the brash way you speak or act; perhaps because you do not display a particular skill ... there could be numerous objective or subjective reasons.

To ascertain what these are and to work on these is the positive step of self-improvement. The alternative is to whine, complain and condemn ... an act of self-degradation.

There could of course be the situation where you have become an unwitting victim of some employment quota policy. This need not be as unusual as one thinks.

In Malaysia, approved companies are required to have a workforce that at all levels reflects the racial composition of the country.

In America, Canada and other countries there are similiar provisions for "equal opportunities" or "affirmative action" whereby a deprived group is given an opportunity for upward mobility by law or policy.

You are deserving of a promotion but someone else has been placed above you either because of the above policy or because he just happened to be the favourite of the boss. This person, now your superior could be better, equal or lower in capability than yourself.

Whatever the situation you have a choice — to leave the organisation and seek greener pastures or to continue to work. If you leave, the problem ends there. But if you continue to stay, you can either fill yourself with the cancer cells of discontent and destroy yourself or you can work for your own self-respect, your own sense of self-pride.

Work and make yourself indispensible to the person above you. Thus when he moves up further you yourself may also move up.

When even such prospects do not exist, work for your own sense of self-satisfaction. If nothing else, then at least you will be happy with yourself and that is a happiness that is often difficult to come by.

If you start a campaign of character assasination of non-cooperation, then understand that "as you sow so you will reap." And as you try to bring down others, others will equally try to bring you down.

Negativity breeds negativity in as much as positive actions attract positive actions.

To put this on a spiritual dimension "Hate attracts Hate. Love attracts Love. Peace attracts Peace." Be in Peace!

Fault — Finders

Non-Violation

Fault finders

The world is full of "fault finders"! Is this too pessimistic a statement? Perhaps you think that you are free of this disease of fault finding? Well, let's examine this subject.

Let us recall the earlier example and look at the picture and see how relevant this may be in daily life. Today the child is sitting on the floor, enjoying his book and drinking some orange juice. The mother passes by, does not see the cup and accidently knocks it. At once she admonishes the child "You fool! Is that the place to put your cup?"

She then continues, "Go take a cloth and clean up the mess." The admonished child duly complies.

The next day, the mother is relaxing, resting on a chair, reading a ladies magazine and enjoying a cup of coffee. The cup is placed on the carpet. The child rushes into the room, eager to share some great news with mum. He rushes forward "Mother!" Mother ...," he does not see the cup and kicks it and coffee is spilled on the carpet.

The mother reacts "You stupid child, can't you see where you are going? ... Go take a cloth and clean up the mess!"

The child was deemed wrong in both instances and the mother did not think that she was at fault — for not seeing the cup in the first instance or for the cup being on the floor in the second instance.

Was this not the very characteristic of man that caused a great soul, many years ago, to declare: "He who is sinless, let him cast the first stone" ... and no stones were thrown.

Also "we are able to see the mote in the eye of another — but not the beam that is in our own eye" ... and thus it goes on, the great teachings of the world warning man not to be a fault finder. But has man learnt ... have you learnt?

If we want to find faults, we can do so with anything, any product, any activity, even with things of nature — of God's creation! For example, here are some faults we can find with God — "Why did He create the Sun so hot? Why could it not be a nice mild temperature?"

"Why is the rose so fragile?" "Why does the orchid not smell like the rose?" "Why did God create some rich and others poor?" ... thus it can go on, and we can make our life totally miserable in the process.

However, it is interesting to note that it is the small mind that seeks to find faults and points out disparagingly the weakness in others. Great minds only look at what is good and noble in others, recognising that there is good in all. If they do find faults it is with the view to correct and assist, rather than to demean and condemn.

There is a story of Gautama Buddha that is perhaps illustrative of the greatness of man's mind. Buddha was walking along the road with his disciples and other followers and they came across a dead dog! As they passed the dog, the disciples began to comment one after another "what a filthy sight", "what a terrible smell", "look at the worms", "look at all that dirt", "look at those filthy flies" and thus it went on, all expressing disgust at the dead animal.

Buddha kept quiet for a while and after all the comments had subsided quietly remarked, "What beautiful white teeth the dog had!" Amidst all the dirt and decay he had seen beauty.

Thus is the nature of high Human Values, to be able to see what is good and noble in all! However, what we sometimes have today are the small minds who are able to pick only the faults within any activity or work, however noble it is.

Let us all look at ourselves in our home environments, in our relationships with friends and relatives. How quick are we to find faults with the habits and behaviour of others? How often are we ready to find faults the behaviour of our friends and relatives' children while we ignore the gross misbehaviour of our own children? Thus it goes on — some never appear satisfied; they are constantly grumbling about this, that or the other ... and thus plant mental seeds of discontent that can destroy their peace of mind.

How do we go about pulling out these weeds of discontent? We shall examine this in the next chapter and we will also go into the office or work environment and see if we can identify the fault finders there.

Encourage — By seeking goodness

Do we have anybody reading this who has a similar type of situation as that portrayed in the picture? You could be the boss or you could be the subordinate. Someone has put in a lot of effort into a piece of work. However instead of looking at the content and quality of the work itself, you pick on a spelling mistake i.e. on the peripheral factors of the completed task and kill the enthusiasm of the person who has undertaken the task.

It is quite likely that almost all of us have either been in the situation of the aggressor or the aggrieved during some part of our working life.

Here again is the difference between the great mind and the little mind i.e. one who has imbibed and is practising Everyday Human Values and one who, by not being conscious of EHV, has degraded himself in the eye of his subordinate and any other independent observer.

On the subject of Fault Finders — the world can be divided into four groups of people viz:

(1) Those who try to seek their own faults, however small these may be, try to correct these faults and only look at the good others do.

(2) Those who look at the good in themselves and the good in others.
(3) Those who only look at the good in themselves and only at the faults in others (and try to demean the one making the fault).
(4) Those who consider all their negative qualities as positive factors and condemn the good that others do.

I must hasten to admit that the above rather incisive division of human characteristics is not mine, but that presented by Sri Sathya Sai Baba in attempting to help man look at himself — see the absurdity of his actions or behaviour and hopefully improve himself.

Our effort of course, as we imbibe high Human Values, is to move from the fourth position to the first.

Does that mean, as we move up the ladder of human consciousness, from the base to the noble, that we should ignore the faults and mistakes of others? Not by any means!

To be on the highest level of human consciousness, at work, with our friends, relatives, and colleagues, is not to ignore or gloss over the mistakes of others.

We should in fact be ever vigilant of the goodness and the faults and weaknesses of others for often it helps us to aspire for that same goodness and to recognise the same faults within ourselves. However what is more important is how we choose to point out the weakness or errors and what our motive is.

The pointing out of error should never be done with the view to demean or condemn. It should be done with love and concern, ensuring that there is no loss of face, and with that person being fully aware that you are doing this only to help them to improve and become better.

Your methodology will of course be seen and felt by others, but often, your motive, only you will know and thus you exalt yourself or demean yourself to your own conscience.

Let us look at the picture again. One practising EHV in his life would have first praised the worker for his effort, and then gently pointed out errors of facts or interpretation. As for the spelling mistakes he would have laughed at these and asked the subordinate to watch out for the printers devil or these typists and their carelessness. This would have brought the best out of the worker.

Normally it is only a person who has an exaggerated opinion of himself or someone trying to compensate for his own inferiority or merely someone with an inferiority complex, who will attempt to find faults to demean others.

Usually someone who is confident of himself and his own ability will rarely resort to cotton picking — finding every little fault in others. He is concerned with broad direction, the real content and not so much the form of any activity or work. If mistakes are made he realises that a word of encouragement together with a gentle reminder to be careful can be more effective than angry words or sarcasm.

On the other hand someone unsure of his own ability or with a complex problem will always try to compensate for his own weakness or sense of inferiority by coming on heavy on work undertaken by others. He will find the smallest faults and exaggerate these so as to assert himself.

Such people usually miss the woods for the trees, get involved in minute unessential details, rather than the issues and thus dissipate their own energy on non-essentials while at the same time dissipating the enthusiasm of others.

Does the cap fit? Do you see yourself? The first step in upgrading Human Values and one's own self esteem is to recognise one's weakness. Once this is recognised then correction can be made and only then can we elevate ourselves.

Good luck!

... "Go on! Make a monkey of yourself ..." — for once —

Non-Violation

There were once three wise monkeys — see no evil, hear no evil and speak no evil. Man was enamoured by the great virtues, the great truths that the three wise monkeys portrayed, and thus he began to immortalise these three monkeys in print and as wooden, metal , plastics and ceramic figures.

The three wise monkeys thus entered the books and homes of man — transcending borders of nationality, race, religion, etc.

Today the results of the great lessons taught by the three wise monkeys are evident in the world. All the monkeys faithfully follow these commandments — they do not speak, hear or see evil! Man has happily allowed the monkeys to follow the advice but sadly has not taken the trouble to follow the advice himself.

And thus is the problem of much of the world — at home, among relatives and friends, in office environments, among members in clubs and societies, in government and politics, among government and politicians.

Perhaps the mistake was due to the monkeys themselves, for they forgot to include one other monkey as their leader from which all other qualities arise i.e. THOUGHT. If the monkey that THINKS NO EVIL had come in first, the others would have been more successful in persuading man to follow the good advice.

It is from thought that all our problems arise. If we want to see evil, the negative, we will see only that which is base and debasing. If we want to hear that which is base and debasing we will only hear thus and all our subsequent thoughts and actions will likewise be tainted.

Thus it goes on! A great mind once said God if you think of, God you are. Dust if you think of, dust you are. Verily thoughts are things. As you think you become!

What is the significance, one may ask, of using the monkey to project these values? Perhaps it is because of the nature of man's mind that has often been described as the 'monkey mind'! Why? This is because of the tendency of the mind, which like a monkey, swings wildly from tree to tree, from thought to thought, from idea to idea, from joy to sorrow, from anger to love, etc. It can sometimes be like a mad monkey always chattering, always agitated, always fretting!

It is thus the mind that is responsible at least in the general sense i.e. without going into deeper aspects of consciousness. The eye really does not see, it is merely an organ that allows the vision to enter your consciousness but something else within you really sees. Let us call this the mind. (What causes the mind to see ... this is another subject entirely).

To explain further. How often have you been reading a book, your eyes scanning page after page, but after some time you realise that you cannot remember what you have read? Your eyes were looking at the words on the pages but your mind was elsewhere. Thus you did not record any of the words.

Likewise with hearing. You often may be listening to some lecture and if it is boring, your mind wanders and you do not record anything that is being said.

Thus also with speech. A slip of the tongue being no fault of the mind — how often in a moment of anger or emotion have you said things you did not really mean to say?

It is thus not your eyes, ears or mouth that is responsible for receiving or projecting negativity. It is the mind! Once we control the mind (negative thoughts), then we control all the other organs of action and this brings us to the fifth monkey ... DO NO EVIL!

So let us all go on and make a monkey of ourselves for once — let us try to follow the advice of the five wise monkeys — Think, See, Hear, Speak and Do No Evil.

But it is easier said than done.

How do you control the leader of all the monkeys — the commander-in-chief, Think no evil? Once he begins to behave himself, all the other monkeys will follow suit and eventually you will have a peaceful, harmonious and relatively happy life (barring of course tragedies and other events that could disturb this harmonious balance).

We will examine this subject — how to control Mr Think No Evil in the next.

EVERYDAY HUMAN VALUES
SEE NO EVIL
DO NO EVIL
SPEAK NO EVIL
THINK NO EVIL
HEAR NO EVIL
THE 5 CHILDREN OF IMMORTALITY

Non-Violation

In the last chapter we talked about the five wise monkeys — Messrs THINK, SEE, HEAR, SPEAK and DO NO EVIL. We also identified Mr "Think No Evil" as the Chief culprit — the leader of the band, who if not brought under control will make all the other monkeys (our sense organs) misbehave themselves.

We also recognised the fact that, it appears that in the main, only monkeys are following the advice of the five wise monkeys ... but not man.

Thus let me now introduce to you — not monkeys — but five Children of Immortality.

As "the child is the father of man", let the immortal message of goodness that these five children convey help man in his search for Peace, Happiness and Harmony, and ultimately the type of immortality that his belief or religion promises him.

But now the key question: How can we control Mr Think No Evil? How can we control this monkey mind, the incessant thought process that often robs man of the peace of mind he seeks?

All of us are only too aware that verbal silence is not silence at all. Our mouths may not be moving but thoughts will be screaming, screeching, moaning, complaining, chattering endlessly, even robbing one of sleep! What can we do?

Various methodologies have been introduced over time to help man quell the vagaries of the mind. Imagine the mind to be a monkey. Left on its own it will run helter skelter! However if like the organ grinder you give the monkey some specific work to do, then you gain some degree of control.

What work is this?

Let us look at our mind again. What happens to you when you (i.e. your mind) gets angry, agitated, sad or fearful? At once the rhythm of your breathing is affected. There appears to be an irrevocable link between the state of our mind and the rhythm of our breathing. Even when we are happy, joyful or victorious, the breathing is disturbed and we begin to breathe faster or more deeply.

Thus if the agitation of the mind can affect our breathing, can the reverse be achieved? Can our breathing process affect the state of our mind? Yes, it most certainly can!

However like the monkey belonging to the grinder, that goes up and down the pole to attract a few coins only after a lot of patient training, so only, with patient training can the "monkey mind" be brought under control.

To do this you have to initially train the "monkey" in an area where there are no disturbances or distractions. Choose a quiet place a quiet time of day. Sit up straight, imagine your spine to be the pole along which the monkey must go up and down and thus keep it straight.

Even as you sit thus, quietly, with no external provocation, your mind will not stay in one place. It will begin to take you to all your problems, your office, family, friends, your desires, your hates, your loves, etc. Now is the time to start the training process.

Begin breathing gently but deeply. Using your diaphragm, feel the air go into your stomach, i.e. instead of your chest coming out when you inhale, feel your stomach virtually bloat. Then when you exhale, let all the air be expelled. Draw your stomach in. Make sure your breathing is rhythmic, i.e. if your breathe in for five counts, breathe out for five counts. Do not artificially strain yourself. Let it be as natural as you can.

While this is going on, what should the monkey mind be doing?Fix your attention on the tip of your nose. Place a watchman on your nose and as your inhale, let your mind follow the air into your lungs and when you exhale, let your mind follow it out. The monkey is now given a task to perform — clambering down and up your spine following the passage of air.

After some practice you will find that during this period no extraneous thought has come to your mind and your mind thus having rested, will be recharged.

Once you have mastered this breathing process, at least to a degree, and when you are able to do this spontaneously you will find this a useful tool to calm mental agitations during the day.

You may get angry with someone or something, you may feel insulted, hurt, you may feel agitated and overwhelmed with work, or some sorrow may be driving you crazy. At once go to a quiet place even just your office chair, bus or car seat — anywhere. Sit up straight and start breathing rhythmically, evenly, bring your breath under control and give work to the monkey mind to follow your breath in and out. You should find the results startling. It will not overcome the problem but it gives you a chance to recoup, to pause — "catch your breath" so to speak — so that you are in a better position to tackle your problems.

There are of course other methods and techniques that can be used to control the mind. Often our mind is like a flood light and thus when we do a piece of work we are unable to get the best out of ourselves because the mind is unable to focus. Imagine the kind of control you can have on your life, on the quality of any work you do if you are able to focus your mind like a laser beam and cut out extraneous thought!

Various techniques of mind control — silent sitting, meditation, prayer, etc. — have been taught over the centuries to give man the capacity to control his thoughts so that he "thinks no evil"!

For those readers interested in the subject of meditation, I have produced a booklet and an audio tape on the science and methodology of meditation presented in a totally non-sectarian and universal manner. This tape and book can be obtained by writing to "Meditation tape" No. 24, Jalan Abdullah, Off Jalan Bangsar, 59000 Kuala Lumpur, Malaysia. The cost is US$2.50 (minus postage). The proceeds go to service activities undertaken for the needy.

Sow And Reap

There was once a woman who gave birth to a beautiful boy (child) and he grew to be the "apple of her eye". He was up to all types of loving, amusing, childish pranks. The mother used to take him along shopping and as he loved it, she would carry him on her shoulder.

One day a vendor of tit-bits and nuts was passing by, his wares balanced on a tray on his head. The child grabbed a packet of the nuts and the vendor walked on, blissfully unaware of this childish caper.

The mother of course was tickled pink at the way in which her child had taken the packet of nuts without "being caught". This became the topic of conversation with friends and neighbours as she hugged her child lovingly. The child was equally pleased and began to repeat this performance at every opportunity ... "to please mum".

When the age of understanding and discrimination dawned on the child, the youth would now of course conceal these innocent pranks from his mother. He began to thrill at his ability to deftly pocket goods from shops, etc. And now he had the adulation of his friends to urge him on. One thing led to another and he began to concentrate on bigger and more valuable items, more challenging adventures.

As you sow

So shall you reap!

One day, he and his friends, "only meant to take the jewellery from the jeweller's shop", "no harm to anyone" and then the stupid watchman — "the old fool" had to show up. Just like in the movie the young man hit him on the head to silence him ... not to kill ... they meant no harm ... but ...!

Well the young man got caught and was finally sentenced to be hung for murder. As the time approached for the execution he was asked for his final wish and he replied "I want to see my mother". Very moved by the filial piety of the young man the authorities brought forth the aging, sorrowful mother to her child. When she was near, the young man leaped forward and attempted to choke her, screaming: "It is all your fault! It is all your fault! If you had checked me as a child I would not have ended up like this!"

A sad story indeed of misguided mother's love, ... a story borrowed from a speech of a spiritual teacher. If all of us look at the story itself, it has very little relevance to our daily life as parents or elders ... "our children have never been encouraged to steal".

However if we look at the "inner significance", the message behind the story, then we will see that the little story screams a message, a warning to all parents and elders.

How often have we seen parents visiting a friend's house with their children and allowing the children to abuse or at least treat badly the property, furniture, children or (children's toys of the friend), while the poor friend (or especially relative) suffers in mental anguish not wanting to say anything to hurt the friend's feeling.

Often parents appear hesitant to reprimand their children in front of friends or relatives, the child sensing this can often exhibit misbehaviour patterns that he or she would not display at home.

Parents and elders also often abuse each other in front of their children or they condemn and talk ill of their friends, relatives, or worse, they condemn a man's religion, a race or a class of society. The child absorbs all this like a dry sponge and it could well be squeezed out one day in front of the parent at the most embarrassing moment.

A child may come home from school and brag to his parents, elder brothers or sisters how he had slapped a friend for calling him names or how he had returned abuse for abuse. What would your reaction be as an elder, a parent, uncle, elder brother or sister? Would you give the child a pat on the back and praise him for his "macho" behaviour, for teaching the other fellow a lesson? Would you sharply reprimand your child (physically or verbally) for indulging in such hooligan type behaviour? Would you sit down and talk to the child of an alternative mode of reaction for any such future situation?

What you do in situations such as these or other similar situations could plant the seeds for the future behaviour of the child, could affect his behaviour patterns, his relationship with his peers, his self-confidence, his relationship with others, etc.

Parents, elder brothers or sisters, uncles, aunts, elder friends and relatives all can impact positively or negatively on the future behaviour patterns of children. Thus very thoughtful behaviour, thoughtful actions and reactions in front of children are recommended.

You can hide the truth from everyone except your own conscience and god

From Where Do You Hide Truth?

"Tell the truth and shame the devil" ... this is an old saying. But why and how can one shame the devil by speaking the truth? In much of Eastern philosophy or spiritual thought, truth is equated to God. And a person upholding truth under all circumstances is said to be giving expression to the God factor within himself.

Thus it becomes a beautiful synergy of Eastern and Western Values and Spiritually when we understand that if God is Truth and Truth is spoken, automatically the Devil cannot be present. He is "shamed" (so to speak) and cannot affect us.

But who or what is the devil we speak of! The West has given us the image of the devil with tail, long eared, a red garment and holding a pitchfork or trident. The Eastern concepts also have similar invocations with long sharp teeth, demonic features, etc.

However there is another perception of the devil that all can and should have and that is the negative and "demonic" characteristics of man. There are a host of these "devilish" or devil prompted qualities including anger, hatred, lust, jealousy, pride, backbiting, fault finding, etc. These are the devils and they exist within man. It is a moot point for us to worry if the devil exists in another environment called Hell!

Whatever our belief, if we can get rid of the demonic qualities, the devil in us, then we can be assured that there need not be a subsequent tenure for us with the devil in another environment or another dimension of existence.

In the picture, the gentleman (could be any one of us) has already given in to one demonic trait, i.e. backbiting, talking ill of another behind his back, now he is reinforcing the negative by perpetrating a lie and thus continues the vicious cycle of value degradation in man.

He steps into one negative quality and to reinforce, hide or justify that one, he perpetrates another. He comforts himself that his friend will not know what he has done, little realising that he himself, his conscience is aware of this (and often it is said that conscience is the prompting of the Divine in man) and this has the potential of robbing him of peace of mind and sometimes even sleep.

If one believes in God, and that God is omnipresent and Omniscient, then this alone should make one aware that there is no such thing as hiding falsehood, either from oneself or a higher force.

Often we tend to tell what we call "white lies" as if there are a whole range of colours or at least shades of black and white. However man can be comforted that there are circumstances under which such lies, one may call them white because they cause no damage or harm, can be uttered.

When wanting to tell a truth, as we perceive it (after all, often, truth is one's own perception of an event or deed), if that truth could cause more harm, ill feeling, degrade others, etc. then it is better than the truth be unsaid.

In the circumstance of the picture, after having precipitated negativity by backbiting, our friend could have taken the noble option of telling the truth, apologising for talking ill or at least given his reasons why he talked ill, thus giving his friend a chance to explain.

This would have helped to in fact bring their friendship closer and the friend would have appreciated the honesty. However, having taken the negative alternative, the gentleman will always be haunted by the fear that one day his friend whould find out the truth and this will most certainly destroy the friendship.

Friendship like a beautiful plant can only grow in the sunshine of love and honesty, and also the ability to accept and give criticism without rancour. We will look at this further in the next chapter.

THE VALUE OF FRIENDSHIP

The Value Of Friendship

A friend in need is a friend indeed.
For what are friends for?
As a staff to the lame,
as a tent in the rain.
A true friend is life's greatest gain.

Sadly however, as precious as is this gain, many find that it is equally rare!

Today we hear of "fairweather friends", a term that really is a scar on the noble face of friendship. One should search one's soul as to the type of friend one is, and the type of friend one has. Are you a "fairweather" friend who is only around when the going is good or can you be depended upon when the going gets rough? What type of people do you yourself spend hours of life with? Will they be around during stormy days?

The picture that accompanies this theme presents a situation which many face during their life. A friend has done something wrong – deliberately or accidentally, consciously or unconsciously. Do you go and tell the friend his fault? Often people take the attitude that "it's none of my business. Why should I put my nose into it and spoil my friendship?"

Such a friend is no friend at all! A friend should be like a pair of spectacles which clarifies the vision, and whether the scene in front is "dirty" or "clean" it does not hide the truth. It merely, without fear or favour, reveals the truth and allows one to make a decision based upon this truth.

Watch out for the "flattered friend" who tells you all that you would like to hear. In many ways an enemy is more useful for your own personal development. He (the enemy) will search out your faults and having revealed them to you at least gives you a chance to correct yourself. A famous South American guerilla fighter once cried out: "God please protect me from my friends. I can look after my enemies."

A gain many mistake a good friend as someone you can approach to borrow money from, and if he does not lend you the money he is no friend. In fact it is such financial transactions between friends that have spoilt beautiful friendships and even caused ill-will amongst blood relations. Do not ask your best friend for money. And if you do lend that money be prepared to accept that his may have to be a gift. If not it is better to refuse gently rather than cause bitterness in future.

We have many friends. Who then can we take the courage to correct, without the danger of affecting friendship? It is a friend who knows instinctively that you genuinely care for his/her welfare; and it is a friend who realises that your advice on a fault is not do demean and discredit, hut to correct and elevate. You must have conducted yourself in such a manner in the past that the friend knows that all these qualities are in you. Such a true friend is indeed a gift.

Oddly enough sometimes one may find that it is not the person whom one considers as one's best friend who comes forward to offer unsolicited advice which you know instinctively to be true. Whatch such people who pass through your life, you may be allowing a diamond to slip away while holding glass baubles in your hands.

Many can easily cry and share the grief of a friend, but find it more difficult to cry with his or her joy and happiness or good fortune. If you find that you can without any scruples feel the thrill of inner joy at the happiness, good fortune and success of a friend then indeed you are a good friend to have around!

MONKEY: THE ANIMAL

MAN: THE MONKEY MIND

The Monkey Mind!

"Oh Mind! How can I still your wayward ways?

Oh Mind! How can I trek your secret ways?

You have the power to drag me down to darkest days.

You have power to lift my life to glorious ways!"

It is said that when man was created he was given a deadly, two-edged sword. This is the mind. It has the power to cut away the bonds of sorrow and mental pain, and it has also the power to bind and to cause harm to its user (if not well used).

The mind is man's greatest friend, but it can also be our greatest enemy. In the first instance bringing joy, peace and contentment and in the second causing pain and agony. What is the cause? How can we learn to use the mind as it was meant to be used, for the elevation of man through the acquisition of the highest human values and ultimately wisdom (as different from knowledge)?

As mentioned earlier the mind is often compared to a monkey, sometimes a mad monkey, given its propensity to swing wildly from limb to limb, from thought to thought, without the ability to remain in one spot, to concentrate on one thought over any length of time and thus give respite to the heated (or overheated) mind of man.

There is a quaint story as to how monkeys are caught in some countries. The villagers adopt a very simple strategem. They place some nuts into a very narrow necked vase/jug and leave it in an appropriate area. The monkey comes along and places its hand into the jug and grasps a handful of huts. It then finds, that it is not able to take its hand from the jug.

The villagers approach the monkey and it flees taking the jug with it. The terrified monkey perceives that something or someone is holding its hand inside the jug. It does not realise that its freedom could be obtained by just letting go of the nuts. It desperately tries to climb up a tree, but hampered by the jug it falls easy prey to the villagers.

The mind of man is like this monkey. Man's mind is assaulted by a hundred worries of the past, present and future. He is unable to forgive or forget past or present conflicts, quarrels, problems and thus carries this burden every day from home to office and to other places where he collects more worries. He is then unable to sleep, the monkey mind clutching desperately at the worries. To forget the worries, to relax, he takes cigarettes, liquor, sleeping pills, stimulants, seeks the company of false friends, etc. He even puts the hand of his monkey mind into the jug of future worries and drags himself to despair while outwardly often feigning happiness and bravado.

(Doctors and psychiatrists live well on these poor fellow humans). All they have to do is to let go and the worries will not haunt them through their lives. The particular problem will not disappear, but the ability to let go and not to carry the worry of office to home, or vice versa, will give the mind a chance to rest and recuperate and thus give the individual added strength and ability to face the problems of life.

But this in itself is the greatest problem i.e. "how to let go?" How to still the vagaries of the mind? How to detach oneself from a problem and tackle it at the appropriate time and not go be overcome by the problem?

The ancients used the technique of meditation to gain mastery of the mind. Today, because the word meditation smacks too much of an Eastern or Indian tradition, new words have been coined and the rose is thus called by other names ... mind control, Bio-feedback, dynamic thought control, silent sitting, etc. The unfortunate and mistaken association of meditation with a particular religion has deprived many from benefitting from this blood-pressure reducing, mind consoling technique. It is as though all of the East would reject aerobics as an exercise for physical health because a Western Christian introduced it!

If one is able to use discrimination and realise that worrying about a problem will not solve it or reduce its impact, this could help in a way to encourage the monkey let go of the nuts. Or, at least a few of the nuts. Such a process of enquiry would be a useful adjunct and could become part of a preliminary process of silent sitting or meditation.

Place a ceiling on desires and open yourself to inner peace and happiness!

Ceiling On desires # 1

"Desire" — the storm that whips one to frenzy.

"Desire" — the whirlpool that drags one to despair;

Why do you wish to hold me in your arms oh Desire;

For your looks or touch I do not care.

Two friends, both very successful, having all the material and external trappings of success and happiness — wife, cars, houses, directorships in companies or senior positions in Government, members of Social Clubs, etc. Both find that all the accumulation of wealth, position, influence, etc. do not have the power to give them inner peace, inner happiness or contentment.

Now they both have to decide a future course of action to secure this inner peace and happiness. One has decided that the path for him is to acquire more — more cars, houses, directorships, membership in social clubs, and the like and thinks that the accumulation of these externals may give him the inner peace and happiness he seeks.

The other has decided to take a directly opposite route. He has decided to place a ceiling on his desires for the externals and to concentrate on seeking the path of spirituality and using his time and money to serve the sick, the poor and the needy, i.e. to try to bring happiness to others!

Now the question is: "Who Found Happiness?"

Readers who are in different strata of society in different positions in life may wish to just put the book down for a while and reflect on this question within the context of their own lives.

Desire has been described by someone as akin to "fire". The more one feeds a desire, the greater its power.

Thus desire feeds on itself, growing larger and larger, demanding more and more until it leads to the destruction of the one who tries to satiate desire by feeding it.

The prisons, the cardiac care units, the mental institutions and the "suicide" files of police records are filled with names of people who tried to satisfy desire by feeding it and ultimately became victims of their own insatiability.

All the religious and spiritual teachings of the world are replete with warnings to man about the danger of "Demon Desire". The great teachings of the world are designed to help man avoid these great pitfalls of modern life and to help man journey comfortably through life till he reaches his "promised destination".

"It is easier for a camel to go through the eye of a needle than a rich man to enter heaven" was surely not a phrase to discourage man from striving to satisfy his basic needs and comforts of life, but to warn against the unbridled pursuit of wealth, name and fame, forgetting the codes of righteousness and morality.

Did not another great "light" of the world caution that the cause of sorrow in the world is Desire and gave man the path of "moderation in all things" i.e. the Middle Path, if we want happiness and peace and to avoid sorrow!

"Simple Living, High Thinking" has been the call to man for all ages, but man has instead chosen the path of "high living and low thinking". And this has led to a world obsessed with excessive materialism and the degradation of Human Values.

The "keeping up with the Joneses" syndrome is perhaps the best manifestation of the ills of modern society. It is most peculiar that man wishes to only keep up with Jones in pursuit of what is external, often superfluous, and ostentatious.

How come there is not a singularly strong desire to keep up with those who are spiritual, loving, caring, sharing?

If man aspired to keep up not with the Joneses, but with the great advice given in the spiritual texts of world — the Holy Koran, the Bible, the Dhamapada, the Guru Granth Sahib or the Bhagavad Githa. If every person tried to keep up, and in fact strove harder than his neighbours to live their lives according to the teachings of these great "neighbours" of ours; if all men tried to place a "ceiling on their desires" and **searched for wealth within**, man would have opened the door for not only his own happiness, but also for the happiness of the poor, the sick and the needy!

How are we to place a "Ceiling On Our Desires?" What Desires should we place a ceiling on? What Desires should we acquire? We may discuss these in the next section.

In the last section we talked of the need to place a

EVERYDAY HUMAN VALUES.

Ceiling On Desires # 2

"Ceiling On Desires". When one talks of this Ceiling On Desires one does not refer to the **elimination** of all desires! As long as the human body exists man will be bound by Ego and Desire.

Thus when one talks of the destruction of Ego or placing a Ceiling on Desires, it is with the objective of reducing the negative or destructive aspects of Ego and the excesses of Desires, often also termed as "lust" for money, power, privilege, sex, etc.

What desires should man focus on, i.e. to limit, and to transform to good use for the benefit of the individual, and society? In examining the gamut of human desires, perhaps for the purpose of developing Everyday Human Values, one may wish to focus on placing a Ceiling On Desires on MONEY, TIME, FOOD, ENERGY, KNOWLEDGE.

If one is able to focus on one or more of these, one will find that automatically all other excesses will gradually come under control! Let us examine each of these and their implications on our lifes.

The acronym for Ceiling On Desires is COD, and one will find that by practising COD, if one is able to "deliver" this in one's life he will end up saving or improving also cash, character, comfort etc. — a truly "Cash On Delivery" programme.

And if one places a Ceiling On Desires Everyday, this can become a CODE for life, to reduce unnecessary worry and problems that man strives so earnestly to earn!

Let us look at the various components of this CODE.

C eiling

O n

D esires

E veryday

COD or Money. To say that we must not desire money would be to close the gap between floor and ceiling on normal living itself. Money is a necesity, but how it is obtained — righteously or unrighteously is the question!

Even if it is earned righteously, then the headlong pursuit of money with the negation of other qualitative, humanistic aspects of life will render man an inert machine, bringing inner joy neither to himself or others.

Many spend their lives accumulating wealth and then die of heart diseases, stress, or simple burn-out, and find they can't take anything with them beyond their grave or funeral pyre. They leave an inheritance to children who often, even if they do not squander the wealth (thanks to good financial managers) spend their lives seeking pleasure and thrills and ending up being of benefit neither to themselves nor to society.

Alexander the Great, who conquered a good part of his known world, but alas not himself, is purported to have told his generals with his dying breath: "When you place me on the funeral pyre, place me with my open palms facing upwards, so that all may see that though I have conquered the world I take nothing with me" — a flash of spiritual realization during the final moments with Destiny.

Money should be earned, and even lots of it, but righteously. And such money should be used not to fulfil excessive desires, but to serve the welfare of mankind. Such a person is blessed not only in living but also in life hereafter.

For those who are not very wealthy in financial terms, how can we practise COD with money. Very simple, you can spiritualise this effor by cutting down expenditure on all your negative or less productive pursuits. If you are smoking two packets of cigarettes a day, reduce this to one and place the savings of expenditure on the other into a piggy bank for the needy.

Likewise if you drink excessively, reduce and use that for the needy. Likewise going to movies, renting video cassettes, buying countless dresses and shoes, etc. reduce unnecessary excesses and save that money for the less fortunate.

Thus COD on money is not merely a savings programme testing your propensity to save, but a dynamic human value elevation programme where you benefit by reducing the negative and wasteful in your life and the savings so derived benefit the needy.

If one tries it for one or two years, with patience and persistence and if you not merely save the money but also make an effort to personally go to the needy who are benefiting from your savings, you will derive immense satisfaction in life.

Do not be concerned that the quantum of money saved because of your denial of the negative is small. It does not take much to buy some food or delicacies for poor children, the orphaned or aged. But it takes much love!

COD on Time. Someone once said that "Time Is Life" and that "God Is Time". Thus one who wastes time is in fact wasting life and is offending Divinity itself. Modern society has created for man a host of time wasting devices that are threatening to sink much of society into a morass of lethargy.

Look at your own home and identify the **"life stealers"** in your environment. The **"idiot box"** the TV, and now the deadly accessory to the idiot box, the VCR. All these not only steal our time and lives but also deaden the mind and sap the energy of children, youth and adults.

This is by no means a call to dump TV's or VCRs into garbage cans, but most certainly a call to re-examine our lives and the lives of our children and their relationship to TV. Today Governments have to launch special reading campaigns because excessive TV has eroded the "reading culture" in modern society.

The bars and discos of the world are other stealers of time, encouraging a waste of money, the destruction of health and morality and creating a negeration of "fast living". Many fail to realise that excessive fast living ... is the fastest way to ... an early grave.

One must ask oneself: "Is this necessary? What benefit does it give to my life, my living, my family etc?" We should differentiate between what is merely pleasurable and what is beneficial i.e. that which brings satisfaction and joy, and then take appropriate action to adjust our lives to echieve this lasting happiness and joy.

If you are able to place a COD on Time, then the next question is: what do you do with time on your hands? Look around you with a new perspective of selflessness and you will find the answer. Your children most certainly need more of your personal time and attention.

And there is a difference between a parent who just stays at home for long hours but spending no time with children and one who takes an active interest in the children, their work, play, interests, etc.

And if that has been satisfied, numerous social service organisations exist that do not want or need your money but will welcome your time to be spent with the orphans, the sick, the poor and needy!

Thus we have a programme of Ceiling on Desires on time and money! What about COD on Food, Energy and Knowledge? Well this we will look at in the next section.

Ceiling On Desires # 3

There was once a revered holy man who had renounced everything and was living the life on an ascetic. God decided to test his renunciation and created for him a gift of a mountain of gold. The holy man smiled and said: "My Lord, is this your test? As I have renounced the material world and seek only spiritual wealth this mountain of gold has no attraction for me.

However my Lord, if I had been filled with worldly desires, surely this one mountain of gold would not have been enough!"

For the last two chapters, we have talked about "CODE of life", the Ceiling On Desires Everyday for Everyone. In the last we raised the issue of COD on Money, Time, Food, Energy and Knowledge and discussed at some length the COD on Money and Time. Now let us look at the rest.

COD on Food. This may be self-evident to most and this is a classic case where desire fuels desire. Man just eats too much, often too quickly of the wrong food at the wrong time and in the wrong amounts.

The health clinics of the world have most certainly had the ceiling of their bank balances raised because of man's inability to place a COD on food.

Everything in moderation — Excess in enjoyment can lead to excessive pain!!

But the practice of COD on food goes beyond just eating too much. It calls for a drastic ceiling on the sheer waste of food. Someone once said that perhaps half the hungry population of the world could be fed everyday by the food that is wasted by man.

At home, in parties, cocktail gatherings, restaurants everywhere, food is cooked in excess and then dumped into waste bins. If some sort of retrival system is available, at least animals could be fed on this rich food (which could well be bad for the animals themselves). The rest ends up in dustbins and waste heaps and become fodder for flies, rats and scavenging creatures of the night.

Parents will be well advised to teach their children to respect food. The reintroduction of the lost culture of saying grace and praying, thanking God for the food before one eats would benefit the family.

Some traditions take God as food as it is responsible for our very survival, and thus to waste this God or Gift of God is a grievious sin. Needless to say parents will have the difficult task of setting the example themselves. However once the initial hesitancy or shyness is overcome, this pre-food prayer will become quite a compelling and useful habit.

Also such a habit of not wasting food generates savings for the family that could be used for the needy.

COD on Energy. This could be a self-evident COD, but not once we think about it.

Children should be taught, and again adults should set the example, to turn off taps so that tubs don't overflow, switch off lights, fans, air-conditioners and the like when one leaves the room; turn of the TV and radio when no one is watching. All these are manifestations of the wasteful society and it is an indictment of man's consciousness that Governments have to step in to remind us not to waste electricity, water and energy.

Then there is the similiar waste of energy in other environments like offices, where, since it is not our own, more waste is manifested. Hotels have to impose automatic lighting systems that are activitated by room keys, simply because the appeal to the guest to switch off TV and lights when they leave the room falls on deaf ears, for — "After all I am paying for it — so why should I bother to help them (the hotel) save money?"

Thus it goes on! Waste of man's physical mental and spiritual energies in activities that are harmful to himself or totally unproductive to the individual or common wealth are too numerous to be elaborated.

We should all reflect on these and adjust ourselves so as to live in harmony with ourselves and Nature.

The destruction of environment is another collosal waste of the nergy created by nature over thousands of years. Can man continue this destruction of eons of concentrated energy? Should not every individual do his or her bit to help?

COD on Knowledge. The enigma of all: why should there be a COD on Knowledge? The answer is simply in knowing oneself!

Look at what you absorb into your mind through your organs of perception, especially your eyes and ears. How much of what you read everyday is fit to be remembered and cherished as useful to life, and how much of it can be relegated to the dustbins of our life? Yet it goes on.

Man absorbs through the electronic and print media, knowledge of things, events and people totally irrelevant to his or her life. He absorbs all this "knowledge" of the love and sex lives of the famous, infamous, high and mighty; he takes in sensational, exciting stories through the eyes and ears and makes his brain the garbage can for every piece of rubbish which editors, publishers and the film producers churn out to satisfy the lower instincts of man.

Here is a test you may try yourselves. You receive a newspaper and a number of the frontpage headlines call for your attention — "Rape in the Park", "Adultery in High Society", "Brutal Murder in the Streets", "Government urges greater Productivity", "Holy man calls for faith in God"! Which of the news items would more than 90% of the readership lap up with alacrity, as if their lives depended upon their reading this news?

One can almost predict the format of their reading — "Rape", "Adultery", "Murder" and ... well the Government's call ... perhaps. And what does the holy man say "Ah ... same old thing, don't bother".

Thus man begins to read and accumulate knowledge and information that in fact insults his higher and finer instincts. It is said "as you think ... you become", and most certainly much of what we think is influenced by what we read and hear.

If all our inputs are debasing, our thoughts will naturally be equally affected and this will be reflected in our words, attitudes and actions! "Garbage in ... garbage out", is true not only for the computer.

One may ask: What then about ceilings on other aspects of life? Reflect on the "basic five" and one will find that all others will be modulated and affected by these! If adults have no inclination to follow this CODE, then at least for the sake of our children and the society of the future we have to make an effort to introduce these into our own lives, the lives of our families and eventually to friends, society and the Nation.

A society that is able to manifest this Ceiling On Desires Everyday (CODE) as a national consciousness will surely benefit and prosper. But it starts with each and every one of us.

PRACTISE WHAT YOU PREACH

Right Conduct

"That's why I want you to know.

I'm starting with the man in the mirror.

I" m asking him to change his ways.

And no message could have been any clearer.

If you wanna make the world a better place.

Take a look at yourself and then make a change."

Not many readers would realise that the above highly philosphical statement is an extract from Michael Jackson's song, "Man in the Mirror". It is a moot point as to whether Mr Jackson practises what he preaches or is it just "Don't do what I do. Do what I say!" It is equally a moot point as to whether he composed the lines or merely sang the words all the way to the bank!

We are not here to see if others benefit from words of wisdom. The critical question is: "Do I benefit? Can I as an individual make the change?"

Take a look at the doctor in the picture (it need not be a doctor but just a friend). The hollow ring of this advice is obvious to all. But, let us not be too quick to pass judgement on the good doctor. Look at ourselves in the mirror of our conscience and reflect upon the advice we have generously showered on others, but would have benefitted tremendously ourselves if we ourselves had lived by them.

The mother who screams at the child to "stop screaming!" (Some do not merely stop at verbal battery but resort to violence in order to "Get some peace!"); the father who preaches against the follies of a thieving habit, but proudly displays "souvenirs" from hotel rooms, aircraft and even pencils and stationery from the office; the teacher who complains about declining standards of academic excellence but is himself/herself shoddy in lesson preparation and presentation, are all part of a generation of "Do as I say ..." elders.

Values must be cultivated not "taught". So one has to have them, before one can attempt to transplant these values to others.

This reminds one of a wise and respected man who was approached by a mother of a boy who loved eating sweets (to the detriment of his teeth and gums) to advise her son against taking sweets. The wise man looked lovingly at the child, patted him and told the mother to return with the boy after two weeks. Dutifully the mother returned on the appointed day anxiously waiting to hear what advice the good man would give her son. The old man looked smilingly at the boy and said: "Son, don't take sweets in future. They are bad for your teeth." That was all he said.

The somewhat disappointed mother confronted the wise man when they were alone, and said: "Why! You could have given him the same advice two weeks ago. Why did you make me go and come back, only to say those very words which I myself have told him so often?"

The wise man replied that as he himself had a sweet-tooth, he had no right to advise the boy against taking sweets then. But since seeing the boy the first time, he had refrained from his usual "sweet indulgence" and now this self-imposed discipline had given him the right to advise the boy against sweets.

Needless to say, the child listened to the words of the wise old man.

There was no miracle in the words that the wise man spoke. The sentence he uttered was the same one the mother and other good intentioned persons had constantly badgered the child with. Yet none of these had had any effect. Only the advice of the wise one touched the boy. Why? Because together with the word was the "Force" — the life force of "being" — BEING an example, a living force of the word. The wise man "became" the words he spoke. He earned the right to advise.

A man of truth is he in whom his thoughts, words and deeds are one. The renowned American sage, Emerson puts it this way: *"Do not say things. What you are stands over you all the while, and thunders so that I cannot hear what you say to the contrary."*

So if you are someone advising a friend on something you yourself obviously do not practise, remember, "What you are stands over you and thunders" so that your friend cannot hear what you preach to the contrary.

We look into the mirror on the wall to see if our hair is in place, our mascara is not smudged, our tie straight, etc. But do we look into our "inner mirror" to see if we like the person within. So next time you stand in front of the mirror, don't concentrate only on the superficial, cosmetic impact. Look into the mirror and remember: "If you want to make this world a better place take a look at yourself and then make a change."

Do unto others as you would like others to do unto you

Do not do unto others what you do not want others to do unto you

"Do Unto Others ..."

Values spring from the mind of man and manifest in action. Occasionally we hear of great and noble deeds that capture the imagination and one is then reminded of the need to adhere to and uphold values. However, whereas a singular act of nobility may be inspiring or bring praise and kudos to the manifester of the values, it is the **value we maintain and manifest in the hum-drum of daily life** that spells **the difference between a life of internal torment** and dissatisfaction **or** a life of **inner joy**, satisfaction and peace.

In the picture we see the classic situation in all urban cities — that can bring about the worst or the best in us. The person in question is you ... or me!

You have an appointment and it is 8 a.m. or 9 a.m. — a time when most people arrive at work! You have arrived also. The parking bays for visitors are a bit far away, and who wants to walk in the sun anyway. You are only going to be away for a short while!

If it had been 10 a.m. or 11 a.m., then it can reasonably be assumed that the owner of the parking bay has gone for a meeting and it is likely that your act may not be a selfish one. You thus can park in the bay with a relatively easy conscience and pray that the owner of the bay does not show up.

However, at 8 a.m. or 9 a.m. in the morning (or even at 2 or 3 p.m. in the noon) one cannot, without selfishness, assume that the owner of the bay will not turn up. Those who do not must ask themselves, "what if I was the owner of the bay, how would I feel?" Whereas one can symphathise with the plight of another, to emphathise is a more dynamic process to virtually place oneself in another's shoes. It was this internalisation process that the great minds of the world were trying to manifest in man when they gave the advise: "Do not do unto others what you do not want them to do unto you" and conversely. "Do unto others what you would want others to do to you."

Now the shoe shifts to be other foot. The owner of the bay arrives. He is filled with chagrin that his place has been violated. What should he do? The following are several options.

(a) Park his car in front of the offending car and block his exit. The danger of this is of course that you may tend to block the neighbouring car also and thus become the "aggressor" yourself.
(b) Park your car elsewhere and either scratch the paint or empty the air from the tyre of the offending car (a more conspicous, lower form of retaliation).
(c) Park your car elsewhere and place a note of the offending windscreen "Please do not be selfish" or words to that effect.

What one does is often a reflection of the value that one holds, as part of his life. Ancient Indian behavourial sceintists have identified 3 "Gunas" (behaviorial, attitudinal or emotional qualities) of man.

They called if **Rajasic** (the aggressive, hot tempered or activity orientated) Guna, **Thamasic** (the dull, lethargic, tending towards inertia) Guna, or **Sathwic** (balanced-peaceful, contented) Guna. In modern western parlance these perhaps could be the extrovert, introvert and balanced personalities. We will examine this in relation to EHV later. For the time being, it suffices to understand that all human beings have within them all the 3 Gunas, with some having one Guna more predominant in daily life.

In the context of the "car situation" — the Rajastic dominated personality would probably puncture the tyre! The Thamasic personality would probably park his car in front of the offender for he/she would find it too bothersome to park it far away and to walk back. Such a person is oblivious to the inconvenience caused to the other neighbouring car owner. The Sathwic dominated personality would take the 3rd course of action and even probably think "the fellow possibly had an emergency" and let it go at that.

It is interesting to reflect (and readers may measure their own reactions or those of their friends) that the type of reaction manifested in this car situation will probably be the reaction that the person manifests in other environments, at home, office, among friends etc.

If one does not like the kind of value that the characters in the pictures depict — one may wish to reflect on one's own ways. We carry our values on our shirtsleeves (or blouse sleeves) and sometimes it can be an ugly sight! Let's all start washing our individual sleeves and soon we will find others doing the same! Even if they don't, it does not really matter — a sense of personal satisfaction will prevail when we do something we know is right — that should be reward enough.

Money is the root of evil, and opportunity leads to temptation

"Opportunity Leads To Temptation"

"Money is the root of all evil" — what a trite, often used, often overused statement ... and thus, with **"familiarity breeding contempt"** (again an overused statement) — man tucks these immortal messages into the archives of unused thoughts and goes on repeating the same mistakes and thus goes on suffering the consequences of his own neglect.

"What fools these mortals be!" — (another often used phrase) — but did the bard know a secret that is denied to the rest of mankind? Man (and here I do not exclude the female of our species) seems terminally addicted to committing the same follies of his forefathers, and incredibily, even after being "once bitten" acts none the wiser for his plight.

Readers will note from the drawing that I have chosen to drop the "all" from the phrase and have just said "Money" is the root of all evil! — for it is not money but the mind of man that is the root of **all** evil. In this context, it is the misuse of money that is the problem. Perhaps we should rephrase the message and say "MISUSE OF MONEY IS THE ROOT OF ALL EVIL". Man of course has the capacity for prepetrating evil without money coming into the picture — but that is another story.

What is the human value message in this context? Could the bane of modern society be the working parents? Both father and mother work in high pressure enviroments, both plunge themselves into the rat race of modern society to satisfy their individual ambitions, and they both give what they quaintly call "quality time" to their children — the children are given "quality money" to spend and needless to say such quality money does not come in single or even double digit denominations.

The child is thus given a financial strength far beyond its ability to discriminate on its proper use — even many adults have this problem. The child wins friends and respect. The child becomes a kind of leader in his/her environment and needless to say the peers who wish to exploit the child can take easy advantage of this naiviety and false sense of values that the parents have inadvertently given to the child.

Not only can this financial strength lead to misuse — cigarettes, pornography and perhaps eventually drugs — there is another damaging effect this has on the other peers of the child (in school or in the neighbourhood), who do not come from wealthy families or whose parents are more circumspect with money they give their children. Feelings of inferiority, jealously and envy. are created in others and unwittingly other children are also drawn into negative value orientation by the ostentatious display of money by their peers.

By the time the parent becomes aware that the "quality time" they spend with the child does not compensate for the vast amount of low quality time the children spend with their "quality money" — it is often too late.

All children, however naughty they may appear to be basically like to be considered good, and given love and understanding (and this takes time) they will tend towards goodness. However, until they develop a strong willpower, and a fine sense of discrimination they are open to all kinds of temptations ... and it is **opportunity** that leads to this temptation.

Many parents, in trying to justify their own action will say "Oh! I trust my son or daughter" and the innocent faced child will probably smile and nod in assent! But what is the basis of this trust? What values have the parents implanted in the child to place this sacred trust in his/her own hands. To give a child a gun or knife without teaching the child proper respect and safeguards for its use and to say, "I trust my child" is to abuse a parental prerogative. Likewise with money or other trappings of power and wealth! If the child has not been nurtured with the proper values — the gun may one day go off — by accident of course, and when our own child or others get hurt — it is too late for tears, accusations, or even self-recrimination.

Let us all watch our children and even ourselves — and dust the old proverbs and sayings from the archives and give them a fresh perspective in our lives.

LOVE LIVES BY GIVING AND FORGIVING -
SELF LIVES BY GETTING AND FORGETING.

Love And Self

Love Lives by Giving and Forgiving. Self Lives by Getting and Forgetting — Baba —

A statement made by a great spiritual light and worthy of study, reflection and implementation in all our lives.

The essence of all human values is LOVE. Not the selfish love that tends to discriminate or limit the value of love; not the love that is often a guise for lust, but a love that is universal, unselfish ... shining on all with equal splendour. Like the sun that shines on all without discrimination, like the sun that smiles on those who curse it and those who praise it, so is the potential for universal love that is in the soul of man. This gentle love that gives and forgives is among the divine qualities of man and has the power — like the gentle water that creates gorges in the harsh land — to transform hate to love.

There is an interesting story associated with the Holy Prophet Mohammad that has always caught my heart. It was at the time when the Holy Prophet was conveying God's message of Love, surrender to God, discipline and devotion in an environment that was hostile to the new religion. It is said that the Holy Prophet would take a particular route in the city everyday to reach his place for prayer. Along this route there was a particular lady who was angry at the Holy Prophet for preaching this new religion and to show her displeasure she would wait at the upper storey of her house and as he passed by, would throw some rubbish over him.

The Holy Prophet would not react, he would merely brush off the rubbish and proceed on his way. And everyday he would have this rubbish thrown over him and everyday he would brush himself and walk on.

One day as he passed by the house, expecting the usual shower of rubbish ... nothing! He paused and no rubbish showered forth. Curious at this absence of aggression, he went to the door of the offending home. He knocked and called out for peace and found the door unlocked. On entering the home he found the elderly lady very sick and helpless, with no one to care for her. The Holy Prophet attended to her and would visit her daily with food and medication. The lady recovered and became a devotee of this new religion whose founder reflected so much the Love, Compassion and Peace that he was preaching.

The Holy Prophet was thus an example of the vivifying force of the statement. "Love lives by Giving and Forgiving." If all people of the world can live their lives by this call which is merely an expression of what is already the basis of man, the core of his reality, the world would be a wonderful place.

I have no way of knowing if the story above has a historical basis or is part of the legend that builds around great personalities. However, knowing the power of God's Love that the Holy Prophet must have manifested in his daily life, I have no reason to doubt that the incident could well have taken place.

However, today man has chosen to forsake his birthright — the right to love. He has forgotten that he himself is a creation of love, an expression of love, that he was fostered by love and grows in love. Man has chosen to restrict that pure unlimited love by selfishness, by narrowness, by the imposition on the unlimited love the limitation of "I" and "Mine". Thus we have today many who give life to the statement "Self Lives by Getting and Forgetting".

Many in society today talk merely of "what's in it for me?" "How can I rip off the other guy?" "How can I get more by giving the least?"

Man has forgotten the great sayings of old that have acted as beacons of light for a noble society ... "It is better to give than to receive." They have forgotten that the one true religion of God is ultimately the religion of love and that universal love is the highest manifestation of God in man.

The great religious and spiritual lights of the world not only preached this love, but spent their lives building this mansion of love by daily practice. And the power of that love has lived through centuries and will continue to live. Those who have chosen to grab, to "get and forget", have brought not only sorrow to themselves and to others, but have been relegated to the garbage cans of history.

One of the spiritual leaders of modern times Sri Sathya SAI BABA has provided the following thought as a guide to man on the universal power of Love:

Love as thought is Truth
Love as action is Right Conduct
Love as feeling is Peace
Love as understanding is Non-violence

All men must share in this precious heritage of selfless universal Love and develop it by practice in daily life.

All of us should examine the inner significance of this statement, and its application in daily life.

The Value Of Love II

"LOVE as Thought is TRUTH
LOVE as Action is
RIGHT CONDUCT
LOVE as Feeling is PEACE
LOVE as Understanding is NON-VIOLENCE"

In the last section we examined the inner significance of the value of love as manifested in thought, word and deed.

The manifestation of Love as action through Right Conduct was expressed in the saying adapted from Jurisprudence "That Justice (Love) must not only be done but must be seen to be done."

Often people take love for granted ... and this starts at home and spreads to the office and other environments. After some time some parents feel a lack of need to show or demonstrate Love to their chidren (after all they know I love them?); adult children fail to demonstrate Love to parents (same reason — after all they should know my feelings); husbands and wives after several years of marriage do not feel the need to demonstrate Love to each other and thus it goes on, to friends, relatives and colleagues.

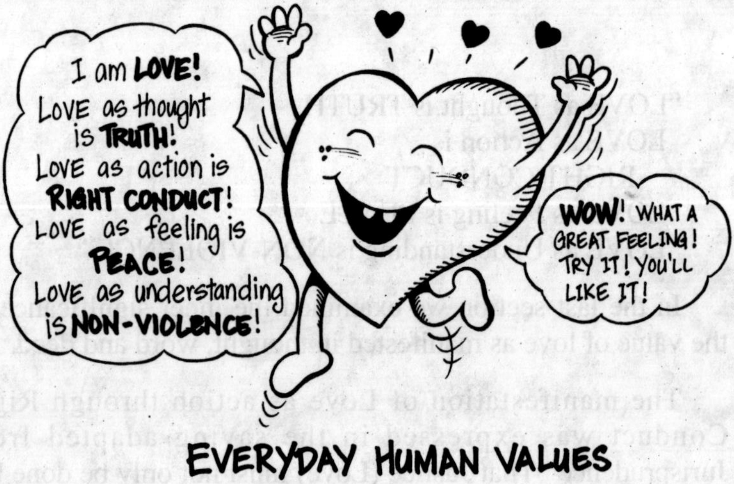
I am LOVE!
Love as thought is TRUTH!
Love as action is RIGHT CONDUCT!
Love as feeling is PEACE!
Love as understanding is NON-VIOLENCE!
WOW! WHAT A GREAT FEELING! TRY IT! YOU'LL LIKE IT!
EVERYDAY HUMAN VALUES

This is a great error and perhaps it was this realisation that prompted the saying: "Familiarity breeds Contempt".

Love is like a plant, a beautiful plant where the leaves are love and where the flower is peace. This plant of Love and Peace must continuously be fostered and cared for with the waters of Love. If this "water" ceases to nourish the plant — it stands the danger of shrivelling up and withering away — unless ... unless of course this plant is able to reach deep down and draw nourishment from subterranean water without need for external nourishment. This would be the case of an individual whose love is so great and universal, whose inner strength is so purified, that he taps love energy within himself, his soul, the Divine in himself. Such an individual is able to give without the need to receive.

Thus it is that love must not only exist — but must be seen to exist through **acts of love — Right Conduct!** Only through words or action will a husband understand the continued deep love of his wife and vice-versa, likewise with the children. Also on a higher plane of consciousness — when people talk of "brotherhood of man" and to "love everyone as your brother" — these are empty slogans unless the love is manifested as action to help our brothers, the poor, the sick and the needy. It is thus that Love as Action is **Right Conduct** or Righteous Action.

Love as Feeling is PEACE From 'Love as thought' which is the intellectual pursuit of **TRUTH**, we have seen love in action at the level of the gross or physical body manifesting in **Right Conduct**. Then we have the emotional domain of the human personality, wherein hate, anger, jealousy and the like drag man to lower, baser emotions and love is lost, where sleep is lost, where you lose your most precious possession — equanimity, peace of mind. However if love manifests at the emotional level it is reflected as a great sense of **inner peace!** Here again, we do not refer to the selfish, self-centred type of love that is related to "I" ness or

"My" ness, but a gentle Universal love for all living things, plants, animals, man, etc.

Thus the greater our unselfish love the greater is our peace of mind — for "love and peace" are two sides of the same coin, as are "hate and mental torment" the two sides of one coin. Which coin you choose to possess is up to you.

LOVE as Understanding is Non-Violence! This is the spiritual domain of the human personality — where your love becomes such a towering light that it manifests in **Non-Violence or Non-Violation**. It is a narrow concept to take non-violence or non-violation at a physical level. When one understands the secret of Life, Truth, Love, Peace, and Right Conduct, one's life becomes transformed in a LOVE that manifests in Non-violation of thought, word and deed — and also Non-Violation of the Laws of God, nature and man. Such a person may be a reflection of William Blake's famous verse:

> "To see the world in a grain of sand and heaven in a wild flower,
> Hold infinity in the palm of your hand and eternity in an hour."

Such a love manifesting as **understanding** — knows that to think negatively is to violate thought; to speak harshly is to violate speech; to harm another is to violate action. Such a person not only merely prays and reads the words of God — but puts these into practice every moment of his life; such a person will not transgress the laws of the land, "giving to Caesar what is Caesar's". Such is the totality of the spiritual equality of Non-Violation as expressed when Love blooms to **Understanding!**

This great value of unselfish love is the core of spirituality and is expressed in all the great religions of the world.

The Holy Prophet Muhammad in **Islam** has said. "You will not enter paradise until you have faith and you will not complete your faith till you love one another."

In the **Bible**, Jesus called on all to "love God" and "Love thy neighbour as you love thyself."

The **Buddha** has said, "The distintive signs of true religion are goodwill, LOVE, truthfulness, purity, nobility of feeling and kindness" ...

"Let man overcome anger by love."

Sikhism says — "On the path of love lies the glory of a 1000 thrones."

Hinduism reminds man that "God is love" and that to "Love and serve man is to love and serve God."

Thus should be the destiny of all those who seek to live a full and glorious life on this earth.

Note: This is an extract of a letter I wrote to the NST in response to letters received from the public who had read the various articles in the New Sunday Times.

"The Holy Prophet Muhammad in Islam has said, "You will not enter Paradise until you have faith and you will not complete your faith till you love one another".

In the Bible, Jesus called on all to "love God" and "Love thy neighbour as you love thyself".

The Buddha has said, "The distinctive signs of true religion are goodwill, LOVE, truthfulness, purity, nobility of feeling and kindness".

"Let man overcome anger by love".

Sikhism says — "On the path of love lies the glory of a 1000 thrones".

Hinduism reminds man that "God is love" and that to "Love and serve man is to love and serve God".

This should be the destiny of all those who seek to live a full and glorious life on this earth.

Note: This is an extract of a letter I wrote to the NST in response to letters received from the public who had read the various articles in the New Sunday Times.

A Response To All Responses

Note: This is an extract of a letter I wrote to the NST in response to letters received from the public who had read the various articles in the New Sunday Times.

I would like to thank all those who have taken the trouble to write in their views on various subjects reflected in my fortnightly column on Everyday Human Values. The fact that some disagree with the high ideals sometimes (or often) expressed is understandable and appreciated. I do not expect total agreement.

One of the purposes of these articles is to create an excitement in the minds of my fellow brothers and sisters on the higher values of life that have often been (in the media) innundated and sometimes obscured by the gross vulgarism, sensationalism, voyeurism and other ideas and writings that tend to cater for the baser instincts of man.

The media of print and airwaves are constantly degrading man himself, let alone human values, by pandering to the vulgar and pedantic. People seem to be excited about negative behaviour patterns, the philandering and love lives of celluloid heroes and heroines, who are often in fact zeros in the values they uphold in their personal lives.

Murder, violence, rape, assault, disrespect for parents, elders and society are often glamourised and grab sensational headlines. The increasing advent of "pulp" literature and pornography is evidence of this degradation of man's higher feelings.

I have asked my friends in the media why they continue to publish "trash" (which they themselves would not want their children to read or be "hooked to") and they have replied candidly "that is what the public wants and so we give them that. If not, we will lose readership and that means losing money". So the public demands trash, is excited about trash and trash is given in good measure.

It was a bold move by the editors of the New Straits Times to allow this column to be published ... for "who is interested in values nowadays?" The written and telephone reactions from readers (regardless whether you agree or disagree with my thoughts) is one of the measures used by the NST to gauge if the public is reading the column.

It was thus a challenge, an experiment, to see if a virtuous cycle of value oriented ideas and thoughts could counter or at least go hand in hand with the vicious cycle of value degradation? Can a fever, an excitement, be created in the minds of the public regarding higher values, which some may not be able to follow or practice but for which all can aspire for, if not for themselves at least for their children.

The readers by their response hane shown that a ripple has been created. Can this become a tidal wave? This again is up to the readers.

It is interesting that among the articles that generated the most response was one on "I WANT PEACE", obviously a subject most relevant to today's complex world. I am afraid some readers have taken an extreme interpretation and position on the subject.

When I referred to the removal of the "I" (ego) and "want" (desire) to get peace, I was not calling for the obliteration of one's ego and the paralysis of all desires.

The human ego can never be destroyed. It will exist till one's last breath. I was referring to the weeding out of the negative aspects of ego, the selfishness, jealously, the self-centred "only me and the rest be dammed" attitude.

I was referring to all that is in one, that you dislike in others. Ego is good and healthy when it expresses itself as self-confidence, wanting to do one's best, to aspire for excellence, in self-satisfaction, self-sacrifice and ultimate self realisation.

Likewise, the concept of "WANT" or Desire. Here we are referring to the negative aspects of desire that manifest in lust for flesh, lust for wealth, power, privilege, recognition, etc. in search of which man degrades himself and destroys those he comes in contact with.

Normal desire is the very impulse of life. To desire what is good, what is attainable by honest effort, sincerity, etc. is noble and should be cultivated in all and encouraged in children and youth.

I am also honoured by the comment of a renowned reader who appeared initially to advocate a position of less than excellence (or idealism) when it comes to expressing oneself, but ended his most valuable contribution by agreeing that honesty is after all a virtue. "It is for us to be careful in our communications so that the expression used will help us to clarify, heal and organise."

That is the excellence in speech that I was driving at.

"We need not always oblige, but we can always speak obligingly. The truth we speak and the righteousness we advocate must not be harsh" are among the excellences that one must seek in life, for harmony and peace.

Another reader in agreeing to the "idealisms" expressed in another article commented very rightly that such great values are part of the Islamic heritage and are the fundamental teachings of the Holy Quran. One must totally agree with this for indeed it is the very purpose of religion to advocate the highest human values and to bring out what is good and godly in man.

I would only like to add to the statement of my Muslim brother, that all the major religions of the world teach and advocate these exact values ... if not, it is no religion.

The fact that the world today is as it is, is a searing indictment on modern man; that while reading the holy books, attending prayers and praising God — he has failed or forgotten to put into practise, in daily life, the teachings of his religion and the highest values of universal love, brotherhood, truth, peace, right conduct, non violence, etc.

It is indeed time for those who believe and more importantly practise these values in daily life, to speak out for these values! We should indeed thank The NST for taking a lead in this.

By the way for those who know me personally and have asked me, my name is legally spelt as J. Jegathesan and I am a government servant and working to promote industrial development in the country.

I pray for equal success in the promotion of Everyday Human Values and Education In Human Values.

Thank you.

Epilogue

Health And Spirituality

All the scriptures of the world urge man to be good and do good. Sri Sathya SAI Baba a spiritual guide to millions in the world to-day,has urged all to "Love All and Serve All" For whose sake? He has said that the **one who serves benefits more** than the one who is served. Is this only for the karmic consequence of the future, for the next life, or is there an immediate more earthly benefit?

This extract from a Scientific Survey Report should be an eye opener for all who wish to serve the sick and the needy.

"Researchers are only now starting to figure out why social ***involvement promotes health and well-being.***

The late Hans Selye, a pioneer in modern stress research, taught that ***by helping people*** *you inspire their gratitude and affection, and the warmth that results somehow* ***helps protect you from stress****. That warm feeling may well come from endorphins, the brain's natural tranquilizers.*

Scientists are also finding that ***good deeds may benefit your immune system****. The mind and immune system are intimately linked.*

LOVE BENEFITS YOU AT LEAST AS MUCH AS THE ONE YOU LOVE!
HATE HURTS YOU MORE THAN THE ONE YOU HATE!
POSITIVE/LOVE ENERGY
POSITIVE/LOVE ENERGY
NEGATIVE/HATE ENERGY
NEGATIVE/HATE ENERGY
POSITIVE/LOVE ENERGY
POSITIVE/LOVE ENERGY
POSITIVE/LOVE ENERGY
NEGATIVE/HATE ENERGY
NEGATIVE/HATE ENERGY
NEGATIVE/HATE ENERGY
POSITIVE/LOVE ENERGY

Neural pathways connect the brain to the bone marrow and spleen, which produce cells needed to fight infection. Researchers have shown that white blood cells are equally sensitive to neuropeptides, chemicals produced by the brain.

In a striking and controversial study at Harvard University, psychologist David McClelland showed students a film of Mother Teresa, the embodiment of altruism, working among Calcutta's sick and poor. Analyses of the students' saliva revealed an increase in immunoglobulin A, an antibody that can help combat respiratory infections.

Whether or not this connection holds up, some researchers believe that your risk of heart disease is dramatically affected by your attitude towards other people. Hostility, they contend, definitely multiplies your risk. Anger, irritability and aggressive competitiveness seem to put people at higher risk for heart disease.

A study at the Duke University Medical Centre at Durham, North Carolina, found that the more hostile the person, the more blocked his coronary arteries were.

In Baltimore, the University of Maryland's James Lynch found that people who do not listen well, who jump at the first chance to answer back tended to have higher blood pressure.

Some will resist the idea that altruism can be good for the self. To profit by doing something nice for someone might seem to cheapen that act.

Still, the reality is that we are first and foremost a communal species, designed by nature to depend on one another. If helping a neighbour is in our own best interest, so much the better."

So my dear Brothers and Sisters, go out and help those in need. You need to for your own sake more than for the ones you serve.

All religions and great spiritual masters have also urged man to "Forgive and Forget".

SAI Baba has said: "There are two things you must forget — the good you do to others and the wrong others do to you." Reading the above can one see any more earthly benefits for those who are prepared to "forgive and forget"?

Is there further proof that one does obtain personal benefit for a selfless act? This is not in reference to benefits in the kingdom of Heaven ... but very, very earthly benefits.

In the meantime, "Love All, Serve All" and "Forgive and Forget", its good for you!